# FIELD BROUGHTON PEEPS INTO THE PAST

BY

N. FREARSON

Copyright © 2020 Susan Bowman

All rights reserved. No part of this book may copied or be reproduced in any form without written permission except in the case of brief quotations in critical articles and reviews.

First Printing 2020

## SIDE LINES AT BROUGHTON HOUSE

Hens were always kept at Broughton House, and sometimes a few ducks, and once even six geese. We reared chickens under broody hens and sometimes by incubator. They provided eggs and boiling fowls. One rather confused fowl, it didn't know whether to be male or female. It used to stand on the back yard step and crow as good as any cockerel, and laid eggs like a hen - it was called Magharry being neither one thing or another. We noticed this peculiar fowl was often missing and only showed herself/himself when feeding time came around. After feeding it would hurry off again. This went on for three weeks, then she brought home thirteen of the most beautiful chicks and was so proud of her achievement. We found her empty nest under the hedge at the bottom of the garden sometime later. She became quite an elegant fowl and later died of old age, but crowed up to her last day. My eldest Brother Dixon kept a flock of very special hens, called Well Summers. They were almost like pheasants, their feathers were so shiny and such vivid colours, they laid very, very dark brown eggs. The ducks had their own duck pond, near the pigsty, it is now filled in, but will still be there. We also had Bantams of different varieties. Rabbits and Guinea Pigs were kept in hutches and had to be attended to, night and morning, also cleaned out every Saturday. Pigs, always two in the style, and they were treated like pets along with the rest of the animals. These fed out of huge stone troughs, and there were a number of these troughs around the back garden to hold water for the poultry. After Shep the dog left us, we had a small black and white Terrier called Jack. He was a smart little dog and a great hunter. Cats, always two or three, were always busy in the garden hunting for mice. I remember one being called Jabey and another Razzickety, another Darkie. They could all catch and kill a weasel, and lots of rabbits and rats from the Lime Kiln field. Their resting time was spent snoozing on a cushion at the end of the big steel fender, they were always put out at night - they could find plenty of warm shelter in the hay.

After the pig killing, a day I always hated, in fact really dreaded, the cellar was full of joints being cured into bacon and ham. I well remember my Grandmother sending me into the cellar to fetch the pigs trotters.

"Oh! Need I go?"

"Go along," Grandma said, and down the great stone staircase, I went.

No lights down there in those days, and all the joints looked so awful in the half darkness. I never could touch raw meat, especially pork, so I made a grab at the wretched trotters and ran back, tripping and falling up the staircase. I threw the trotters to the top and got a good reprimand because they would be bruised, saying nothing about my poor bruised and scraped knees. To this day, I get cold shivers up and down my spine if ever I touch raw meat. Ugh!!

There was quite a ritual on pig killing day. Homemade Elderberry wine was made piping hot in a pan and poured into a large jug. On a tray, glasses were placed, one for the butcher and one for each helper. When the poor beast was dead, the men all stood around and assessed its weight. Then the wine tray was carried out and handed around, and they drank to good curing. I was always missing when the wine was ready for distribution, how I hated the whole business. Even the ladring can smell of boiling water for days after. I never fancied using anything that had been connected with that day, I could hardly bear to touch the back door sneck.

My Brother William Dixon (Dick) was very interested in poultry and kept a flock of Well Summers. One was sent to Newton Riggs, the Research Station, and won first prize for the best layer of that breed over 12 months. The prize was a lovely silver vase - won 1931. All these livestock kept us well and truly busy, cleaning out the huts and putting fresh hay in the nest boxes, collecting eggs, feeding pigs, cats, dog, rabbits, and guinea pigs.

When Great Grandfather Robinson was alive and living at Broughton House, a pet Jackdaw shared their affections. This bird would fly into the house and perch on the edge of the fender. The old Grandfather asleep in his chair, his hand would drop down, and instantly Jack gave it a good hard peck, "Oh Darn Thi", said the old man, not daring to touch it. One day Jack went into the dovecot to steal the freshly laid egg, and my Father was so furious, he fired a shot through the cot and came to tell us that he had shot Jack. But, looking into the cot, Jack was still there finishing eating the dove egg. The bullet had penetrated the cot back and front, but not disturbed Jack. This bird mated with a wild one from Stonydale, and built a nest in the yew tree at the back of the house. Quite a posh nest, it was made of cuttings of cloth and linings it had taken from the workroom bench. It lived to a ripe old age, and we as youngsters had one or two which became quite tame, but not so clever as Jack.

Another interest was beekeeping. My Father always attended to them and we had lots of lovely honey. There are 2 or 3 bee bolhms in what was our kitchen garden. Hives were on Bigland and Hampsfell, but they did not suit my father, the aroma given off when opening the hive had a very unpleasant reaction, rendering him almost unconscious, so the bees had to go.

There was a family of owls. One nested in the fork of the big beech tree, and could easily be seen sitting there from the bedroom window. My friend and I got a ladder and went up to view the nest. It was only a few twisted beech twigs, no hay or feathers, and just two pure white eggs lying there under the sticks. A few failures at bringing out a family, the magpie found the nest and destroyed the eggs, but one year the old owl brought out two chicks. She brought them on to the acacia tree for us to see, and one night during a thunderstorm brought them into my Mother's bedroom window, and stayed there all night. Mother and I were living at the Cottage then, and the inside windowsills were very wide.

Another occupation at Broughton House was cleaning all the brass stair rods. Two double staircases and a smaller one up to the W.C. all had brass rods. It was a very good morning's work, taking them all up, polishing them, before putting them down again. The W.C. was quite something, a mahogany seat and surrounds, a pull up handle to flush - rainwater from the house was stored in a tank above the room. The door came out of The Old Chapel, and, had a red baize cover, it must have been installed about 1892-3 and was one of the first in the district.

Inside the home, all sorts of hobbies went on. Mother was an expert at winemaking from fruit, flowers etc, cooking and baking everything we needed. Twelve large loaves of bread were made twice a week, gingerbread, shortbread, pasties, cakes, and one I remember rather special. This cake was an old-fashioned sponge cake with no fat in it, and the beating and whisking was just nobody's business, it was often served for tea on Sundays. One Sunday the Curate, called Heaton, from Grange called and stayed for tea. He complimented Mother on her excellent sponge cake and took a second piece, "Yes" says Dad "She makes 'em out of wind." Nearly every day someone would call and stay for tea. I well remember one man who came periodically, and after tea always thanked Mother and Grandma for their "Hostilities". We used to have a good giggle behind our hands, if still at the table, we weren't allowed to speak during meals. We were strictly brought up, but how glad I am now, when I see the manners of some.

## THE CHOIR TRIP

Every year, about the second Saturday in June, The Choir were treated to an outing, usually to Blackpool. We young members had saved up for weeks and always had quite a goodly sum for the great day. Up bright and early to get a good breakfast and do the necessary chores, we congregated at the Parish Room. Members were allowed to take parents or friends, so there was always quite a number. We waited for our conveyance, which came from Grange Motors - it was a great creaking Chara-bang, it could be heard chugging along quite a time before it arrived and then it shuddered to a stand still outside the Parish Room. Sometimes two of the vehicles were needed to carry all the passengers.

They each held 26, and we all sat transversely - five in a row - each row having its own door with brass handles, with a step to get in. It had a fold back hood and was upholstered in red leather. Being more or less an open coach, we had to take rugs, scarves and extra coats to keep out the draught, especially on the return journey. It was nearly always fine, and one year had been fine so long my Father said it was sure to break sometime, so take macs and umbrellas just in case. We did.

After arriving at Blackpool, after a somewhat lengthy journey we made a beeline for Jenkinson's Cafe for coffee and/or ices. Then off to the Tower - my Father knew the Circus Ringmaster very well and always managed to have a word or two with him early in the day. By doing so, we were given very good ringside seats en-bloc, it just meant we all had to be at the side entrance to the Tower in extra good time. Anyway, after our visit we all did what we wanted - ladies off shop gazing - the young members and their friends down to the Pleasure Beach, South Shore - we went by tram. We went on almost all the amusements and nearly made ourselves sick at 6d a head each time, returning by tram in time for lunch at Booth's Restaurant 12.30pm sharp. The sea air made us all very hungry, so we all did justice to a good meal - beef, lamb, pork and all the extras to choose from. After lunch, we had a quick wash and brush up before heading off to the Matinee, either at The Opera House or The Winter Gardens. We always saw a first-class show and enjoyed every minute of the afternoon. Then it was back to Booths for high tea, usually plaice and chips, followed by trifle and fresh cream cakes. Another quick wash and brush up and we were out on the seafront again. We had about an hour before meeting at the tower, we would shop gaze buying various items to bring home with us. Mother and I found a high-class ladies shop, not far from Booths, they sold beautiful pure silk blouses, and we nearly always managed to get one each - Father paying the bill with a smile.

The great moment had come and we were all counted up outside the tower. The side door was opened for us, and in we went, we sat in excellent seats and were ready for the evening's performance. Before the Circus began there used to be four singers, two ladies, and two men, they sat in the circus ring and entertained us by singing many of the latest hits. The chorus would be repeated so many times, that we all knew the songs to sing on our way home. Copies sold for 6d each and we always bought those that took our fancy. The Circus really was something worth watching and remembering - all first-class items and artists of all kinds. The costumes were beautiful and the clowns, well, the best on earth I am sure. We got to know one quite well. Doodles by name and he always gave us an extra wave and smile as we cheered him on. Another one was called Co-Co, and many more I cannot remember their names. The last scene was always spectacular. The great circular floor sank slowly and filled with water, making the most beautiful swimming pool. Bathing beauties swam around and the sea lions did their turns with great verve and were great favourites with everyone, old and young.

At last, the great performance was over and we had to make our way back to the chara-bang waiting at Talbot Road Car Park. The latest hit song that night had been "Let it rain, Let it rain, Let it rain", and we had all sang it until our throats were dry.  When we at last emerged amongst the great crowds coming out, we were greeted by a terrific thunder storm, It was raining cats and dogs after being fine when we left the chara-bang, we left our coats and umbrellas in it, so we had to walk, run, hurry, do what you could to keep up with the party in such awful conditions. We eventually reached the car park to find the chara-bang was soaking wet. The hood had been left folded back so everything was sopping wet. Being upholstered in red leather added to our discomfort, I was wearing a white blouse, the dye came off the seat and onto the blouse. I never wore it again. What a journey home, it rained every inch of the way. However, we could do nothing about it, so we all sang our heads off and made the best of a very bad job.  It was early Sunday morning when we at last reached home, we had a hot drink before getting off to bed, leaving all the wet garments and rugs strewn around the kitchen. We were all duty-bound to attend Morning Service at 10.30 am on Sunday, and again for Evensong at 6.30 pm, so we did not get much time to rest from our hilarious adventure the day before.  We all survived and told the tale for many a long day.

Those days seem a long time ago now, but everyone seemed to join in and we were happy and intent on having a really good day.

One year we had a change and went to the Southport Flower Show. All very beautiful but not suitable for a Choir outing of all ages - nowhere to sit down except at mealtimes, we were tired out and never went a second time!

On two occasions we went to Blackpool later in the year - September - so that we could have a trip along the Golden Mile to view the illuminations before returning home. One year, a female visitor in our party strayed from the group of members coming out of the tower and was left behind.  My Father gave instructions that we must all look out for her as we went along the mile at snail speed.  Opposite the tower, someone in the party spotted her on the kerb amongst the thronging multitudes.  The coach driver could not stop, so two or three of the strong young men with us leaned over the edge of the vehicle and grabbed the frightened woman. Never will I forget her entrance into her seat, she was plucked from the street by arms or legs, whichever the lads could reach, one saying he thought the whole concern was going to topple over. Bit by bit she was hauled into the vehicle, not a pretty sight, her much be-bloomered legs being in full view. At last, she was in a seat, she looked as though she had been crying, she sat very still and quiet, never uttering a word all the way home. She was very lucky to have been spotted, so great were the crowds. I think she realised that, for she never dared go again. We proceeded with the tour of the illuminations, before making our way home. It seemed an endless journey, sixty miles at about twenty miles per hour, so it was always early morning (Sunday) when we reached home. Another trip over and once again looking forward to the next.

On one occasion on our return journey, the chara-bang driver took the wrong turn and landed us at Knot End, another length of the vehicle and we would all have been in the water. As there was another vehicle close behind us, it was with great difficulty that we turned around safely.

If my memory serves me right, on this same outing we had all been to Tussaud's Waxworks, and my Father, always ready for a joke, stood amongst the figures in the Chamber of Horrors - first one person, then another eyeing him over - then he gave the biggest wink you ever saw to two young women, they gasped, gazed and made off at great speed.

## THE GENTRY

Starting at Broughton Lodge - Mr & Mrs. Ridehalgh, their Son Master George, and two Daughters, Miss Marjorie and Miss Mary, all lived there when I was a girl. They had a full staff of servants inside and out, and all attended Field Broughton Church. The two daughters, as very small girls were always taken out of Church just before the Sermon, their Nanny taking them. In those days sermons were preached at great length, nearly always forty-five minutes in length. Master George died during the war. Miss Marjorie married and known as Mrs. Forest has recently passed away. Miss Mary also married, and now lives abroad.

Stony Dale was the residence of Dr & Mrs. Cowherd along with their two daughters, Miss Rachel and Miss Fanny. The Doctor, Mrs. Cowherd, and Miss Fanny had passed on long before my time. Miss Rachel lived alone at Stony Dale, apart from her secretary and servants. They all attended Field Broughton Church.

Broughton Grove was the residence of Sir John Hibbert, he too had passed on before my time, and Mr & Mrs. H. Hibbert came there next, I think. They also attended Field Broughton Church. They employed seven gardeners and a full staff of servants inside the house.

Wood Broughton, the residence of the Riggs family, later known as Grayrigge, died whilst quite a young man. There were two sons, Master Gray and Master Fletcher, along with one daughter, Miss Ellen, they also had a large staff and horses and carriages, like the previous residences they boasted, cars came along later. They all attended Field Broughton Church.

Broughton Grange, was the residence of the Ravenscroft Family, quite a family of sons and one daughter - Miss Ethel, she later became

Mrs. Ridehalgh, they also employed full staff and carriages, and later cars.

Broughton Hall was the residence of Major and Mrs. Young, a very stately military man with a very dear wife. She was extremely popular in the Parish and especially at Newton School. Twice a year Major and Mrs. Young would visit, much to our delight, no lessons and an early close!
This household gave lovely staff parties with a "favour" for each lady there. Mrs. Young became ill and passed away, the Major soldiered on with his Indian Valet, Rango, and his staff. They also had carriages and horses, later cars, and all attended Field Broughton Church.

Broughton Bank was the residence of the Newbolt family. I can only remember the two Miss Newbolts, one becoming the second Mrs. Major Young. I have no recollection of the other Miss Newbolt. They too all attended Field Broughton Church.

Aynsome was the residence of Sir Euan and Lady McGregor and their daughter Miss Eva. My Aunt was a lady's maid, she was there for some time and always spoke very highly of the family. They too had horses and carriages and then cars later, a full staff of servants, who also attended Field Broughton Church.

Aynsome House was the residence of Mr & Mrs. John Remington, they had one daughter I think. Mr. John Remington started the laboratories at Aynsome and they became very famous - now carried on at Kents Bank.

Longlands House, the residence of the Cadogan family, they had a son called Roger. Then after their day followed by Mr & Mrs. Dixon - landowners and farmers. I am unsure about Field Broughton Church attendance. They probably went to Cartmel Priory.

All these houses gave garden parties, which were quite something - boating on the lake at Aynsome, the lake is no longer there, and special stalls, sideshows, and walks around the Dutch garden and greenhouses. They grew beautiful grapes and peaches, and if given one, it was appreciated it very much.

## FIELD BROUGHTON ENTERTAINMENT etc.

Field Broughton had a very good choir and lots of young folk around, so there was always plenty of talent to put on a show, a play, or a mixed concert. These were given in the Parish Room, a stage being erected at anteroom end with steps to assist getting onto it safely. There was always a two-night effort in the winter, along with monthly whist drives and choir socials. My Father and Mr Whinnerah, the village carpenter, who had his workrooms in the downstairs department of the Parish Room, were the first to introduce whist drives in this part of the country. They had been to London to the White City Exhibition and had been introduced to whist by Father's in-laws. A lot of money was raised for the Ulverston Cottage Hospital and for the Church and different charities.

My Father was a great cyclist and used to cycle all the way to Kettering in Northamptonshire and stay the weekend with Mother's people, then cycle back to Field Broughton. He always managed a trip to London once a year to the White City Exhibition, and brought home various gifts - a page stick, a gyroscope, a diablo, and a white fur coat - real fur - for me as a very small girl. This I wore for Church on Sunday mornings, blue velvet bonnet and brown shoes and white socks completed the outfit. I wore them with great pride and often went to Church with Mother and Nurse Yates and brothers - Father of course singing in the choir all his life.

Carol singing was a great feature in the Parish. The choir, all well wrapped up, would meet at Broughton House, 6.30 pm sharp, and off they would go, all around the gentry who had been previously notified of the forthcoming visit. As we all grew older we were allowed to join in. It was great fun, getting the pitch from a tuning fork, and singing out in the gardens. Then the curtains would open and the maid would come out and invite us all into the house. There we had tea, coffee, mince pies and cakes, and a good subscription for the Choir fund.

My Father also belonged to a Minstrel Society, run by Major Rothwell from Storrs Park near Windermere. Mr. Alfred Thompson being the conductor. We used to help get Dad ready for the Concerts, getting the burnt cork to blacken his face and help him into his fancy costume. The Troop once caused quite a stir driving around picking up the members at different spots, in an open chara-bang. I can remember the vehicle arriving at The Victoria Hall in Grange with a load of Minstrels, some people knew who they were, some just gazed and wondered; What was the world coming to!!!

The Choir always had a Christams Party, held in the Parish Room, each member inviting guests, and a goodly crowd came along. A first-class meal was first on the list, followed by games and dancing, until the early hours of next morning.

Looking through some old programmes of The Village Entertainments, I read that the Parish Room was referred to as "The Theatre" when used for concerts. Front seat 1 / 3 , second seats 1/-, back seats 6d. Show running twice. The Gentry used to attend all in dinner dress, things were done on a very grand scale in those days.

## MR WILLIAM HENRY MARTINDALE

  William Henry was known far and wide and known as Bill 'Ent. His family lived in High Newton, but Bill preferred privacy and made a home for himself out of half a boat. It was turned upside down and had a door fixed on the broad end. For years it stood near the Old Smithy at High Newton and Bill lived very comfortably in it. Only once did I get a peep inside, Bill had gone to the local shop and the door of the boat had swung open. All was very neat inside, a single bed in the narrow end, and utensils hung on the walls, the only heat being from an oil stove. It was a very hurried peep, for I could see Bill on his way back. He was a very shy reserved man, and couldn't abide women, but a better stone waller than he, could not be found in the whole district. As a young lad, he helped build St Peter's Church. When the Old Smithy was demolished, Bill had to find fresh pastures and managed to get permission to erect his humble dwelling in the orchard of The Crown Inn at High Newton. He did odd jobs in the district and could dig a garden over in a very short time. He seemed to run everywhere. He spent his last days in hospital and died there, being laid to rest in St Peter's Churchyard. He was a great character and a perfect gentleman, we all had the greatest respect for him.

## A WALK FROM FIELD BROUGHTON TO THE TOP OF BIGLAND (BLUE STONE - ACID GROUND)

In the early days of summer, we used to set off wildflower hunting, and this particular part of the district was extremely rich in the flora of all kinds. First would be the primroses in the hedgerows, along with dog violets, also sweet white violets grew in one certain spot. The first bridge over the stream was a stopping spot, on one side grew yellow iris, on the other some beautiful watercress. We generally picked a bunch on our return journey. As we trudged on we came across meadowsweet and wood betony with lots of lovely honeysuckle in the hedges and one particular field, just inside the gate was lovely yellow toadflax. The next field was of great interest, because, in the hedge grew some yellow plum trees, and we always stopped and had a good feast, knowing full well we would suffer agonies afterwards, filling our pockets with the fruit we set off once more.

In the roadside near the field called "Three Cocked Hat" grew large spikes of yellow agrimony with greater burnet here and there. The second bridge came next, and again yellow iris, primroses, bluebells, etc. on one side, and watercress on the other. Up the hill, we went past Wood Broughton and Broughton Grange until we came to the turning of the road to Green Bank. The large triangle of ground between the roads was an absolute paradise for wildflowers. First of all, we would come across bog asphodes with its beautiful golden pointed spikes, a few bits of pure white cotton grass here and there, a small stream ran through this triangle, and marsh violets and peppermint, pennycress and ragged robin and various campions grew here, also the bladder campion. Trembling grass was here and there and lots of beautiful big blue butterflies played hide and seek with the lesser blue butterfly, tortoiseshell, king george and peacock butterflies in abundance, along with large yellow and smaller white with orange-tipped wings. Also to be found flying around there was the large black and red moth. It was a lovely spot. Next came Sturdy's GateWay, and the first sprays of achillea, with their greyish daisy-like flowers. Across the road, by Townson Hill Gateway grew a good gooseberry bush, so, of course, we had to stop and inspect to see if any were ripe.

Opposite this gateway grew dyers greenwood, a trailing plant very much like yellow broom. In the boggy part of the roadside, we found fly-catching plants, such as sundew and butterbur, lady's mantle, and vetches of all sorts. The next thing of interest was a good eating apple tree that grew in the roadside, so, another feast before we trudged on up the hill. For quite a long way there grew no wildflowers, the bracken had taken possession of both sides of the road. Then there was a space and the first heather, dark purple. Further on was a variety of heaths, the cross leaved, ling, and bell heathers all growing in profusion. As we went along we could hear grasshoppers in the grass, perhaps a cuckoo, and saw plenty of swallows flying to and fro. The rhododendrons made a good splash of purple on the right. Opposite grew pale man orchids with their beautiful scent, and a few spikes of pale pink orchids, lots of lovely wall ferns, and a few bilberry bushes were also scattered around. As we went on we found grass of parnassus with its wax-like pure white flowers. A few stems of purple and yellow loosestrife grew nearby. Before long we would come to Bigland Tarn, just beyond the devil's stone, and if we were lucky, would find some white water lilies. From there to the very top of the hill were masses of bluebells and primroses, wild dog roses and bird cherry, with fumitory and moschatel and corydalis growing in the grass verges. Plenty of bog myrtle bushes grew up there, they had a very pleasant perfume all their own. A few specimens of twayblade were to be found in this area, with their twin leaves and long flower spike with green orchis like flowers, no scent.

All along the edge of the roadside were masses of bird's foot trefoil with their beautiful yellow and orange flowers, lots of creeping jenny and stonecrop on the walls, it was a beautiful spot. Sometimes we would see a deer in the wood, and once I saw a fully grown badger walking leisurely in the middle of the road, it was as big as a good sized lamb. No ends of bird nests were in the bushes, I don't think we ever missed one. Even gulls nests were to be found on The Lots, once a

Curlew, all very interesting and exciting. By now we were beginning to tire, but we just had to go to the very top of the hill and around the corner, from there we got the finest view of the Cumbrian mountains, Coniston Old Man in the centre, and if there happened to be a sunset it was just out of this world. We retraced our steps back to Field Broughton, again having feasts of gooseberries, apples, and plums, no wonder we didn't want much tea! In the ploughed fields we used to find Lapwings nests, and later on, we would see the chicks running around. This was quite difficult, so great was their camouflage, the parent birds flying overhead, and making loud cries of warning. The chicks lay flat on the ground and would stay there motionless until we passed, then the parent settled on the ground beside them.

Another big thrill was to find the first sweet violets, there were a few hedgerows where they grew abundantly, white and blue, and in those days there was no restriction on the picking of wildflowers, so we often went home with a good bunch of these delicate sweet-smelling blooms. There was a good variety of trees in the Parish, oak, ash, sycamore, silver birch, elm, rowan with its beautiful orange berries in the autumn; lots of beech, green and a few copper. As we came back down the hill from Townson Hill, the valley lay out in front of us like a huge patchwork quilt, the fields all shapes and sizes and colours, one, in particular, stood out above all the rest, it was a field of flax, grown for linseed to feed to the cattle. It had the loveliest blue flowers and was the only field of its kind in the district. Years ago, long before our time, flax was grown in the Parish to make linen. As we retraced our steps on the very rough, stoney, dusty road full of potholes, we would pause again at the triangle to see if we had missed anything. One day a large green frog sat on a stone in the stream beside a fine specimen of water forget-me-not. We could see the beauty in that frog, it had great golden beads for eyes and sat there quite still for a while, then made a great leap and was hidden in all the long grass. Often we have seen beautiful dragonflies hovering about, different colours and a very special butterfly, brimstone, also lived up there. Near the Three Cocked Hat grew the large pale mauve campanulas and field scabious. Sheep's bit scabious grew on top of Bigland, and lots of scotch thistles.

A mallard and water hen both had nests on the edge of the stream; and a hawk wouldn't be far away hunting. It would be very difficult to find a more interesting place than Field Broughton. The roadsides were a picture with bedstraw and harebells and the small daisies and yarrow all growing side by side, making it look like a delicate tapestry.

We would arrive home very tired, but well satisfied with our trip, have a meal, and then proceed to feed the rabbits and guinea pigs, poultry and pigs, and take out large buckets full of freshwater to put in the huge stone troughs - this was drinking water for poultry. Also, collecting kindling and coal ready for the next morning. We hardly ever wasted a minute, for we played hard and worked hard. Another flower worthy of mention was the cowslip. It grew in large quantities and was greatly sought after for winemaking, along with the humble dandelion which seemed to be everywhere. Large quantities of hazel trees grew around the fields and in the woods and produced an endless supply of hazelnuts. One or two walnut trees produced nuts also and a Spanish Chestnut tree grew at Stonydale, near the old apple tree, with its big bunch of mistletoe on one side. The view from Townson Hill was quite superb, the church with its gilded weathercock. Broughton House and the farm, some of the cottages in the village, and Broughton Grove stood out quite clearly. There were great numbers of wild birds of all sorts, and once a nightjar was heard making its purring notes in the beech tree at Broughton House. Another strange visitor was the corncrake. It lived in our front field and had the nerve to eat with the poultry, then croaking all night long and keeping us awake. It had a strange way of throwing its voice to make it sound in a different place. It looked something like a partridge, one day we cornered it behind a lime tree, so we had a good view of it. Another nuisance of a bird was a cuckoo, not sure if it was the same one each year or not, but one came regularly into the big beech tree near the front of the house every April for a number of years, and shouted from 2 a.m. until 2 p.m., a full twenty four hours. When it ever breathed was a mystery. I well remember an Aunt coming to stay and she said how she was longing to hear the cuckoo, we told her we were quite sure she would hear her beloved bird. As stated before, this wretched bird started shouting and kept on and on, one of us got out of bed, opened the window, and clapped our hands. There would be silence until the very moment you were gathering your last leg into bed when it would start again. Morning came and Aunt got up,

"Oh dear," said she "I never thought I would ever hear anything like that, I could have wrung its neck quite happily."

It was an absolute nuisance and seemed to live in the tree always. We were always glad when July came and it flew away. Another very interesting bird was the big owl that nested in the fork of this very tree, laying two eggs at a time. She had great difficulty in rearing a family for the magpies always kept a sharp watch out and stole the eggs many times. However, Mrs. Owl did manage to bring out two youngsters one year, and when they were old enough to leave the nest, she brought them onto the acacia tree to show them off, they made a very beautiful picture sitting there. Numbers of swallows came into the valley, but strange to say we never had a nest in our house. The starlings often nested under the slates, and the wrens and robins always nested somewhere in the grounds. A favourite spot of the wren was in a corner above the lintel of the coal house door, and one year laid ten eggs and hatched them all.

A very interesting sight were the glow worms, only seen at night of course, and their tiny tail lights would glow in the darkness. We used to see these on the Hampsfell Road and near Eggerslack Woods. They were strange wee creatures, rather like a woodlouse. It would be difficult to find them on the roads now, though perhaps some could be found in the woods.

Also found in the woods in the Autumn were the fairy cups - a bright red, saucer-shaped fungus, it only grows on dead hazel twigs. These were very beautiful, and arranged on a bed of moss on a saucer were most attractive. In this district an abundance of mushrooms could be found, the early morning being the best time for a good gathering. Blackberries and wild raspberries were to be found in nearly every hedgerow.

We also found rosebay willowherb, mullein with its huge spikes of yellow flowers and woolly leaves. Cuckoo pint or lord and ladies grew everywhere and had very bright red berries in the Autumn. Blue cranesbill or wild geranium grew plentifully, and the walls were covered with lichen and mosses of all varieties. Foxgloves, figwort, and numerous other plants all grew at Field Broughton. In fact, I think one is nearer God's Heart in Field Broughton than anywhere else on earth. A real beauty spot.

## GREAT GRANDFATHER ROBINSON etc

Great Grandfather Robinson was born in Field Broughton in the year 1818. He and his parents lived in a cottage at the entrance to Broughton Grove, not there now. His Christian name was Robert and later he married Ann, they had four children, two daughters, and two sons. One of the daughters married William Frearson and became my Grandmother. She was born in 1850 - Queen Victoria on the throne. Great Grandfather was a giant of a man, he stood 6'8" tall and could hold a yardstick under each arm with great ease. He wore enormous boots and was a very hard working man. In his young days, he used to walk from Field Broughton to Winster, stay so long and work haymaking and harvesting, etc, and then walk all the way back again. Grandma used to say the metal plates on his shoe soles were worn as thin and as sharp as razors. A wonderful old man he must have been, he lived until in his 92nd year, my eldest brother Dixon can remember him.

Grandma spent all her young days in the cottage, attending The Old Dames School, which was situated in Field Broughton Church Yard about midway between the Lych Gate and The Lime Kiln. The Old Dame came to school each morning by donkey and cart. The donkey being housed for the day in a shed at the end of the school, which was only a single-roomed building. Quite a few children attended the school, and when it was demolished in 1882, or just before, The Old Dame took a room at the farm in Head House - the farm on the Newton Road. The farmhouse kitchen was used as a schoolroom, and had a cupboard in the left hand corner, near the fireplace. This was used as part of the punishment for bad behaviour. The pupils were made to stand on one leg with their faces in the cupboard, and had to learn a full chapter from the Bible. Grandma said she had been in the cupboard many a time, but had cheated, changing legs when The Old Dame was not looking, she certainly knew her Bible. I never heard what The Old Dame's name was, or where she came from. Grandma used to tell us stories that her father had told her, one being of The Resurrectioner, a strange man who lived in Field Broughton Parish. He had a large horse and a huge flat cart with rubber tyres on the wheels. He went out at night, horse hooves muffled, grave robbing, the bodies being taken to the hospitals for research work. Grandma never knew him, or even his name, but her Father knew him personally. As Grandma grew up, she left school very young and went to work at Stony Dale, and after being there for a considerable time, was promoted and became the head cook. She stayed there in Dr. Cowherd's household until her Mother died and she was needed at home to look after the family. At 28 she married William Frearson, a master tailor, the wedding being in the Old Chapel, and as the small cottage was now too small, they moved into two cottages known as Lower Dog Kennels, and stayed there for years. Grandma had nine children, all were born at The Dog Kennels. Her husband (we never knew him so never referred to him as Grandfather) had his tailors shop and workroom at Cartmel - a house called Devonshire House, opposite Ye Olde Priory Shoppe, walking to and from Field Broughton every day. Never a very robust man, he became ill and died of pneumonia at the early age of 42. Grandma was left a widow with seven children to rear, two having died in infancy. When her eldest daughter, Margaret was old enough to be left in charge of the house and family, Grandma would get up at 2 am and walk all the way, on the old road, to Kendal. We reckon it would take her more than five hours to do the journey. She would buy materials to make clothing for the children, cottons and thread, buttons, elastic etc, and carry them home in a large basket, again walking the same distance. She must have been extremely tired when she returned home, but she would be up first the next morning to attend to her many and varied duties.

My Father, Jonathan Dixon, was the eldest son, one sister two years older was called Margaret. Father fancied being a tailor like his own father had been, so went to someone in Grange to learn his profession. He was there for four years and said he was never offered anything but cold mutton for dinner, no wonder he wouldn't eat it later on in life. The four years up he went to Ulverston for two years and then to

Kettering in Northamptonshire for another period, and did so well he managed to get to London and served another two years there with Tailor & Cutter. By the time he finished his training, he had met my mother and her family. They lived in Kettering. He brought mother up north to meet his family, still at Dog Kennels. Marriage was in the air and the cottages were wanted by the owner from Broughton Lodge to house workmen, so they had to start looking for another home. Broughton House had been standing empty for four years and was in a poor state inside and out the farmer across the road used it as a storage for anything and everything - wheat, corn, potatoes etc. The garden was overgrown, the drive all covered in grass and weeds and lots of huge trees. Two walnut trees grew so near the house the branches swept the roof, in fact, from the road the house was hardly visible. Grandma and my Father had been to view the premises.

To quote Great Grandfather. "Was just the place for us."

After all, there was a family of nine to house - only the eldest daughter had married and left home. Mother, not married yet, came up to view, what she must have thought about it goodness alone knows, coming from a TownHouse with all mod cons, and this one with nothing but oil lamps, no drinking water laid on, it was drawn from a pump at the back gate. She must have wondered how she would get the place fit to live in, but they all set to and had it suitable in a short while. In 1903 mother and father married and Broughton House was being rented for the time being. The woodcutter was called in and thirty trees were felled in one go, the trunks being taken away and the tops being sawn up and stored for fire bushing.

By 1905 my Father was ready to buy the property and did so. He had already started up a tailoring business before he left The Dog Kennels and had his workroom in the anteroom of the parish room. By now he was living in Broughton House, there was a room large enough to run his business.

He was an excellent tailor and never had a day out of work after he started at the early age of twenty-three until he was forced to retire owing to ill health. He could cut and sew a buttonhole in exactly two minutes and knew exactly how much buttonhole twist was needed for each one. The buttons were sewn on with "Double Thread and

Twankum" and never came off. Twankum being a sharp tug made at the thread of the very last stitch. The workroom was heated by an open fire, burning wood mostly - being cleaner than coal - to heat the great "Goose", an iron for pressing. Lighting was from a carbide lamp. He used to measure people just anywhere in the roads or fields, wherever they happened to be, and could remember all measurements until he eventually reached home, sometimes jotting down on a stone in the wall.

My mother was a very shy, reserved person, but not afraid of hard work, and she had set about the interior making quite a bit of progress. She and Father lived in one of the front rooms downstairs and had the bedroom above. For quite a long time the family remained at nine, then two got married - Robert and Agnes. Great Grandfather Robinson passed away in March 1909. The two younger brothers of father's left home and went to live in Manchester with their Great Uncle - Grandma's Brother Robert - he had huge gardens with lots of greenhouses and propagated various plants, so they got a good start to their gardening career. They were both young and it was the first time away from home. They had the luxury of an evening paper to read.

One evening one of them said "Oh, listen to this, there's someone here been fined for keeping a disorderly house - What! Says he - they know nowt here, they should see some of the country houses - peggy tub in the middle of the floor, sink full of dirty pots, tables never cleared, no, they know nowt here."

I don't know how long they stayed there learning gardening, but both were sufficiently educated in gardening to take on jobs on their own when they left, and remained gardeners all their lives. One stayed in Manchester, married, and set up a business there, only coming home for holidays. The other came to Grange and set up a Garden Centre and shop at Bay Villa. There is a smallish garden centre there now, the rest of Uncle's garden is now a carpark. Elizabeth Frearson married a Farmer and stayed in the district. George Frearson went to the stables at Wood Broughton to learn horsemanship, then changed his mind and came to learn tailoring with my Father. He too spent a period of time at a finishing school in Northamptonshire. He married and stayed in the district. Agnes Frearson was a teacher and taught at Newton School for years, she married at eighteen, then she and Uncle Hebe went to live in Norfolk on Sir Thomas Hare's Estate as an agent.

## MY FATHER'S GENERATION AND THEIR SCHOOL DAYS

My Father and his sisters and brothers all walked from The Dog Kennels to Cartmel School. Ruled by an elderly master, always known as 'Baw-lo' Simpson, because of his shouting and bawling. They went along with other children of Field Broughton village - the Pixton's, the Crookall's, the Grave's, the Benson's, and others, I can't remember their names. One day my Father and his brother, Robert were not getting on with their work, and 'Baw-lo' shouted "Why aren't you two Frearsons getting on?"

Father replied, "Please Sir, we haven't got a ruler." "Share one between you!" roared the master.

So the two brothers cut a ruler in half.

Another day as they left school for home, they decided to walk through Aynsome wood and fields. One of them had some matches and set fire to some dry grass, it quickly got out of control and set a silver birch tree alight. Suddenly, Sir John Hibbert came from the other direction, saw and even helped put out the fire, then gave them all a real good dressing down and said he would report them to the Headmaster. The next day, the whole band of youngsters went to school in fear and trembling, but nothing was mentioned, much to their relief. The following day the same thing happened, and so on from Tuesday to Thursday, and still, nothing happened or been said. Then, Friday morning William, my father's youngest brother, was reading a passage from The Bible for the Scripture lesson, he was reading about the Fiery Burning Bush. This immediately reminded 'Baw-lo' of the incident. "Come out Field Broughton children." he roared, and gave them all a piece of his mind, and a good whack with the chair leg he used instead of a cane! They all had to stay in one hour after school, then trudged home to more punishment for being late. The inhabitants for miles around said they would rather meet an army of Red Indians, than the Field Broughton Bairns.

My Father's youngest sister trained to be a teacher, going to Ulverston each day meant getting up very early and walking to Cark Train Station from The Dog Kennels, then back again at night. She married at eighteen, Mr. Hebes Clark, he was estate agent at Holker Hall, she taught at Newton School for years, and she and her husband lived at Barber Green (where Mr. Jack Rigg lives now,) Hebes got a new post as an estate agent for Sir Thomas Hase in Norfolk, and they left the district. After Sir Thomas Hase died, Hebes took another similar post and never ever came back to the north, not even when he retired. Both he and Agnes died in the South.

My Father's two younger brothers, Robert and William were the next to be married. The older living in Grange, he had a garden shop and garden at the top of Grange Fell on the right-hand side of the road, a double-fronted house was their home, one front room being the shop. The garden stretched right up to the very top of the fell and was a very difficult piece of land to cultivate, as Robert said "One could hardly keep the soil in its place, it was always sliding down the hill."

The younger brother William, (his twin brother had died at 9 months of age) married a nurse and they lived in Manchester, still pursuing his gardening. Elizabeth was next to marry, she married a Farmer and lived locally all her life. She had been head cook at The Old Netherwood in Grange for years and used to walk home on her half-day, and get back again on foot by 8 pm.

George, the next to marry, his bride being Lady's Maid from Aynsome. They lived at Broughton House for a few years, then took a house at High Newton and were there for a very long time. George had gone into the Stables as a boy after leaving school, to learn horsemanship, driving, riding, grooming etc. The Stables were at Wood Broughton. He was there quite a long time, then decided he wanted to be a tailor with Jonathon Dixon, his eldest brother, so he learned the profession, he too went to the same finishing workshop in Northants that Jonathon Dixon had been to earlier. He was still working as a tailor when he married and after going to live at High Newton, it meant a good walk morning and night to Broughton House, hail, rain, snow, or blow he never failed to get there for 9 am and never left until 9 pm. He never carried a torch, and one very dark night on his way home, fell over something very large lying in the roadway, it was a horse that used to get out of the fields and drop off to sleep anywhere! George was much shaken for a few days.

When my father and his brothers were very young the new Church - St Peters, was consecrated by the Bishop of the Diocese, and a very splendid service was held. My Father and brothers (George and Robert) wanted to become choir boys, however, they had not been baptised as infants, their father being a Baptist, believed in adult baptism. So, as the new Church was not quite ready, the Services being held in the parish room, the font, a small wooden one with a lid, still in Field Broughton Church, it had come from the Old Chapel and had been used for years, was in use in the Parish Room. It stood on a wooden pedestal at the top of the stairs, and that is where my Father and his brothers and sisters were all baptised, along with others. It must have been a very moving ceremony, Grandma, then a widow, said they all ended up in tears.

Grandma's husband died of pneumonia at the early age of forty-two in 1884, the year St Peter's was opened. Alas! Now all Father's generation, their husbands, and wives have all passed on to Higher Service, leaving, myself, and my three brothers the senior members of our branch of the Frearson Family.

Grandma Frearson always wore black after her husband died and I can picture her now, a black alpaca skirt, very, very full gathered into a tight waistband, a black silk bodice very fitting, with lots of tiny buttons and holes down the front, a few pleats and a very high collar, finished off with white lace. She always wore a white linen apron.

Her going out attire was a very smart bonnet that had a jet ornament on the left-hand side. This held a tuft of fluffy black feathers, a bow or two of ribbons here and there, and ribbons to tie under her chin completed the headgear. Over her dress she wore a large black cape, very full and long with horsehair braid under the hem, every lady seemed to have this attached to keep the hem clean, black kid gloves and glace kid shoes, she looked very smart. She never attended Matins at St Peter's (she kept house whilst the rest of the family went), but nearly always managed to go to Evensong. As a very little girl, I used to sit next to her, when I was allowed to go, 6.30 pm being rather late to be out, and 7 pm was bedtime at our house. Grandma used to sing the hymns and one I remember well had a verse that went like this.

"Guard us waking, Guard us sleeping and when we die". I always avoided the third line, daren't think of dying.

## BROUGHTON HOUSE AND ITS GARDENS

All the family were very keen on gardening and kept the front garden spick and span and the kitchen garden across the road at the back of the house in tip-top condition.

The front garden had two lawns with rose beds and a wild area where shrubs like prunus, lilac, and laburnum grew. There was usually a dugout circle in which we put geraniums, forget-me-nots, fuschias, crocus, and nasturtians - all making a good show. A big rockery was filled with alpines and the gardens had day-lilies and lily of the valley, lemon balm, polyanthus, violas, and calceolaria. Snowdrops were everywhere. These grew in huge rings all around the trees in the front field. It was a picture in the spring. There were two copper beech trees at the bottom of this area, lime and linden trees down the side road, and green beeches everywhere. Two of the biggest in the district being quite near the front of the house. The lime trees were felled a very long time ago and now grow as huge bushes. The beech trees are now all gone, some blown down during storms and the copper beeches, at least one of them was gnawed by a donkey and pony and died. There are no big trees in the front field now.

One year the Celebration of St Peter's Day was held in this field and I have a photograph to prove it.

The back garden and the plantation, as we called it, were given over to poultry runs and their houses, also a twin-roomed pigsty with a nearby building that housed hay for bedding of animals, and a very interesting little building always referred to as "Down Yonder." It was for the use of the gardeners and outside workers and was a two-seater affair. "Down Yonder" meant at the bottom of the garden and this term was greatly used when referring to this outside toilet. There was a peat house where peats were stored. The farmer used to cut them from the great mosses at Holker, dry them, and cart them home. We always had a load or two ready for the winter to help out the coal.

A small coal house sat in the backyard. It was half cobbled and half flagged and it was a back-breaking job weeding and sweeping the cobbles and awful swilling the flags, but come what may, it had to be done. The garden across the road was laid out in different plots for vegetables of all sorts. We grew everything bar swede turnips. They took up too much room. There would be great rows of peas, broad and runner beans, potatoes, and a marrow bed under the wall next to the bee bolhms.

For a long time, my father kept bees and we had our own honey for table use and sweetening purposes. The rhubarb bed was quite big and next to it were the Jerusalem artichokes. Around the corner bushes of sage and mint grew freely. A large onion bed and lots of parsley, each bed in my very early days was edged with boxwood and this had to be kept trimmed and under control. There were apple trees of all varieties; the Golden Spire, the Brown Russet, the red, soft eating apple, and another we always called the flat apple, owing to its shape. This was the best eater we had. Bramleys and other cooking apples grew near the house and in the field along with Victoria and Orlean plums, loads of gooseberries, and black, red, and even white currants, were all over the place. Raspberries and strawberries too grew in great profusion. During the fruit picking season, we all had to lend a hand so that Mother could jam and bottle the fruits in turn. Then in autumn potato picking and carrying into the cellar to store. We hardly ever bought a vegetable, so much was grown in our garden. Great patches of cabbages and cauliflowers completed the scene.

Quite a large greenhouse was erected in the kitchen garden so that we could grow our own tomatoes and cucumbers and different flowers, carnations being one. These were very beautiful after the tomatoes were over. Huge plants of chrysanthemums were planted where they had been. Not an inch of ground was wasted.

My Father, being a tailor and spending so much time indoors sewing, was always glad to get out into the gardens and greenhouse for a change and relaxation. He loved the heat and was never happier than when he was in the greenhouse. There was always a job to be done, mowing of lawns, weeding of flower beds and the great drive and circular front, pruning of rose trees, and a hundred and one other jobs. In those days Broughton House and its grounds were really worth looking at.

## A WEEK AT BROUGHTON HOUSE

Sunday - up for 5 am breakfast sharp. Animals all attended to and vegetables prepared for dinner. Church at 10.30 am until 12 noon. Back home to dinner. Grandma kept an eye on things while we were away. Soup, homemade, roast beef and Yorkshire pudding, roast and boiled potatoes, and one or two extra vegetables. Always served yorkshire pudding with the first course and a second helping was served with a lovely sweet sauce and sugar. We had glasses of water to drink.

Before dinner, we had all changed into our second-best clothes. After dinner, we washed the dishes and put them all away. Making a good fire in the sitting room for wet, cold days. On fine days we all went out for a walk. Sometimes to the Hospice. Sometimes to the Tops of Bigland. Mother and Dad and the four of us and whoever was staying with us at the time all went on these walks. Back in time for tea at 4 pm. Feeding poultry again afterwards and getting coals and kindling in for the next morning, before going to church again for 6.30 pm. Often, after Evensong, we would have another walk, sometimes as far as Newby Bridge or even Lakeside. We were always tired at night but we were up bright and early next morning, ready for school.

Monday - Washing Day

Mr. and Mrs. Thompson lived at Newton and were both well-known figures in the district. Mr. Thompson being a woodcutter, could fell great trees single-handed. A man of small stature, he always wore corduroy trousers, made at Broughton House, tied at the knee with Yorks. A very large trilby hat, almost like a ten-gallon hat! he smoked a clay pipe and when it was raining this pipe was turned upside down, otherwise, the rain would have put out the lighted tobacco. His wife was a rather short, plump figure. She always wore a navy blue and white striped cotton skirt, very full and tight-fitting along with a blouse with a very high neck. This is where washing day comes into the story.

She came, walked every Monday, and reached Broughton House at the stroke of 8 am to help with the great pile of laundry. My eldest brother was always very upset when she came. He would not allow her to touch any of his clothing and hid them here, there, and everywhere.

One day, with the washing in full swing, Dixon shouted at the old lady, "My Grandma does not do it like that!".
To which the old lady replied, "If thou doesn't hod thi noise, I'll put thee and thi Grandma under the boiler."
She stayed all day and worked hard from 8 am until all the laundry was dry and ironed and usually left to walk home about 8 pm. She would accept her fee of two shillings and sixpence and leave. At this time a maid called May Christopherson was living in at Broughton House and she did endless jobs. I can remember what a happy soul she was. She never seemed to mind how hard she worked or the endless teasing from my father.

The irons used were called "flats" and were heated on the open coal fire. Sometimes the ancient charcoal iron would be brought out and as it was rather slow and stupid at getting hot, it would be filled with the red hot embers of charcoal, these being heated in the fire. It was put outside, the trapdoor left open for the wind to blow and fan the red embers until it was hot enough to use.

Goffering irons were used for anything with frills on and a glossing iron for cold, starched, stiff, white collars. In the summer on a very hot day as the clothes were ironed they were put on a clothes horse and put outside to air. In the winter they were arranged very neatly on the huge wrack above the kitchen fireplace before being put away in drawers.

What a business wash day was! As there was an abundance of hot water, the cellar steps and great curing slabs in the cellar and all tabletops in the back kitchen and flag floors were also scrubbed. Even the baskets got a ducking and were hung out on the line to dry. It was indeed a hive of industry - never a wasted moment. Whilst the flats were out and hot, Mother would go with a sheet of brown paper and iron off any candle fat dropped on stair carpets etc.

As time went on, the mains water now laid on, a bathroom was installed and then later, electricity. What a boon they were. No more ladling of water or filling the endless oil lamps. The whole valley was wired for electricity. The church and parish rooms too, and all the old oil lamps discarded. We had a big brass table lamp but the bowl had become porous so I had it turned into an electric lamp and still use it.

Tuesday - Bread Baking Day

Up early to get the fireside oven hot. Great branches of trees would be pushed underneath to get it going, so to speak. Whilst the bread was baking, Mother would find time to give dad help in the workroom and was quite an expert waistcoat maker and hemmer of sleeve hands. Everywhere had to be tidied up in case of customers calling, steps washed and the rooms dusted diligently every day.

After tea on Tuesdays, Mother would find the time again and sit down and knit socks and stockings for all the male members of the family, even for her brother who often used to visit us. She made shirts and trousers for the boys and lots of my clothes. Dad always made our coats. Mother also made pegged and woollen rugs, the pegged ones being made from "out of stock" patterns from the workroom and took a whole winter to complete, but once made they lasted a lifetime.

Jam was often made on Tuesdays, being one of the less busy days. Marmalade, strawberry, raspberry. Sixty pounds of wild raspberries we picked one year and they were made into jam. Gooseberry, rhubarb, pineapple - that was very good - apricot, blackberry jelly, and blackcurrant for winter.

We didn't preserve apples, always plenty in the apple cellar, but we did bottle lots of Victoria and Orleans plums and damsons. What stocks of preserves we had! We never, ever bought any.

Wednesday - Bedroom Day

Great armsful of rugs brought down and taken into the backyard to be well shaken. All rooms swept with hand brushes, stiff and soft, and a great dustpan to collect the debris. The cleaning took all morning.

The afternoon up to 3 pm was taken up in dusting and rearranging of rugs etc. Grandma never believed in doing any housework after 3 pm and was always washed and changed by that time. Not five minutes to or five minutes after, 3 pm was the time. She usually read her weekly paper of the Christian Herald or wrote letters to her family, or did sewing. She made patchwork quilts in her younger days but I never saw her crochet. She wore glasses, but one pair had sufficed all her adult life.

Thursday

Front and back staircase to be swept, hall and passage with freestone floors had to be scrubbed, left to dry, then swept with a broom. This removed quite an amount of loose, fine sand from the freestone. Rugs and mats put down in place.

Two front rooms to be cleaned and polished and very often a batch of various cakes were made to ease Friday. Always the usual pet feeding and cleaning out of hutches and hen houses and of course piano practice. Never a dull moment in our establishment.

Friday

Flue cleaning and grate to be black-leaded. Bread making again, and cleaning of both kitchens, scrubbing floors, and tables in the back kitchen. The large, oval, oak gate-legged table to be polished and pot rail and its accumulation cleaned from top to bottom shelf. Pastry was made on Fridays, meat and fruit pies etc. Everywhere was dusted every day and kept very tidy. Again the endless piano practice.

Saturday

General housework. Cleaning flags and the cobble-stoned yard, looking after hens nest boxes and all pet houses. Cleaning of brass and cutlery, taps and doorknobs - every door, bar two, had two brass knobs. The knockers to clean - never a dull moment. We worked hard and played hard. Even Grandma helped with the work in the front garden, weeding, etc, and had a good try in those days. The dear old lady was in her 93rd year when she passed on.

That was a normal week in our house. How we ever had time to cope with the endless relatives that came for holidays every year I just do not know, but came they did. The work was endless but we enjoyed it and never took any harm. We were a very healthy family and apart from the odd cold, we hardly ever ailed a thing.

## MISS COWHERD OF STONYDALE

In my Grandmother's young days, Dr. and Mrs. Cowherd and their two daughters - Miss Rachel and Miss Fanny, lived at Stonydale. The doctor being the GP for the neighbourhood. They employed servants - cook (Grandma), parlour and housemaids and two or three gardeners outside. Peacocks strutted about and they had a very grand horse-drawn carriage with a box arrangement at the back to carry his medical equipment etc. He was driven by his groom, Mr. Salt. The latter lived with his wife in a tiny cottage in the grounds. This cottage had an old-world garden with everlasting sweet peas and moss roses growing freely along with lavender, lad's love, and lots of pansies. Above the cottage, reached by an open ladder staircase, was quite a big room and when I was five years of age, started my first music lessons in this very room. My teacher was Miss Cowherd's secretary and organist of Cartmel Priory. He was very strict and not a great favourite of mine. However, I went each week for my lesson and as I grew older he discovered I had a voice, so singing lessons started quite early. When I look back now I realise he was a very good teacher.

Miss Cowherd, now left alone, had two maids living in and a male secretary to run the place. She was indeed a great character. She had no time for the vicar and started a Sunday School for the Broughton children. We went at 5 pm and stayed until 6 pm. We used to sing Gospel songs, accompanied by Miss Cowherd on the American organ, and then build texts from cardboard letters. My letters were more often on the floor than on the dining table and one Sunday I was picking them up when I found a bright penny - as I thought. So I put it in my pocket and took it home. Not daring to show anyone what I had found I hid it until the next Sunday when I took it back, and after some difficulty got it safely back under the table. Some time later, my father was cleaning out his desk and showed us some coins he had saved. To my surprise they were just like the one I had found and so I told my Father of the incident. That Sunday, Father went to Sunday School with us and told Miss Cowherd what had happened.

Her reply was, "Oh yes, it was found after a few days and had been put there to test the honesty of the children."

It turned out to be a gold sovereign. Needless to say I never, ever touched anything again.

As we grew older, we were allowed to go to the magic lantern shows. These were held in the music room above the harness rooms. A collection was made and given to the Bible Society. Miss Cowherd used to walk miles collecting for this society, and was very often seen traversing the roads at night with her candle lit lantern. It went everywhere with her for she didn't mind trudging the roads after dark. Very often I have seen her trying to re-light the candle for the wind had blown it out. Another thing she always carried was a box of matches. She wore all black, a very squashed flat hat with a velvet bow and large hat pin, a huge full cloak, and a long black Alpaca skirt. These had horsehair braid sewn on the inside of the hem, supposedly to keep the garment clean. All I could do was see it sweep the road. The old lady hardly ever wore gloves, said she always managed to lose one every time she went out. Her poor hands were very knobbly and full of chilblains. Despite hail, rain, snow, and wind - the lot - she was always out collecting somewhere.

The garden was very interesting and had some very exotic plants. There were the red Japanese honeysuckle, no scent but huge bunches of brilliant flowers. The almond-scented Gosse which grew near the greenhouse. The giant dodder or "totty grass" which grew in the border near the Alpine strawberries. Lad's love and lavender and a very dainty double creamy white saxiphage that grew in the lawn.

In the greenhouse, sat a very lovely pink rose tree. If it had more than three blooms out at once, Miss Cowherd would cut and give me one. Then there grew staghorn and scented verbenas, all very lovely and well cared for.

Away from the house was the kitchen garden, known as the terrace garden. Sea kale and globe artichokes among the many vegetables grown. The paths were all grass and kept neatly cut by the gardeners and each plot was edged with a very small boxwood hedge. Sweet smelling herbs were planted very near the path so that the long skirts swished them about and allowed the scent to come pouring out. Above the garden was a small wood, where the daffodils and primroses grew in great profusion and a rookery in the trees. Each Spring I would be allowed to go and pick the wild daffodils and always had to go early in the morning, some of which helped decorate Field Broughton church on Easter day. Every Spring when the young rooks were about ready to fly, a "shoot" was organised, guns coming from the neighbouring gentry. The shot birds were collected and put into bundles of six and distributed in the parish. Rook pie being a Northern delicacy. The secret of a good rook pie being, use only the breasts of the birds, stew well, and make a pie with plenty of hard-boiled eggs and a very good shortcrust. I doubt very much whether anyone uses them these days.

Miss Cowherd would take the birds herself and give them away. One day, the vicar called and found her engaged in rook skinning. She offered him a very rookie hand.
She said "He soon left."
Miss Cowherd had a special cloak and hat for the rook season. They were much bespattered with rook droppings, elastic-sided boots completed her outfit.

Christmas came and there was always a party of sorts. We went and received a mince pie and an orange, but to get the orange we had to put our hands into a huge basket full of holly, a prickly business, and one we didn't care for.

At the time Miss Cowherd had another secretary, a Captain of the Church Army, and not very popular with us as children. The former secretary had died whilst riding his motorcycle going towards Lindale. After his death, I had a new teacher, one called Bessie Duncan from Hampsfield. My lessons were at home, no more going out in the dark, which to me was quite something.

Another party was arranged for the Saturday before Easter Day. The dining room floor had been covered with a coarse natural linen sheet and on it were arranged lots of nests made of hay and filled with numbers of dyed eggs of all colours. In the centre of the arrangement was an empty nest that was to receive fresh eggs taken by the scholars and later distributed around the parish. We were all allowed to choose three of the coloured eggs and promised not to touch them on Easter Sunday, then Easter Monday we went back to Stonydale to roll these eggs on the lawns.

The large music room was approached by a flight of stairs and at the top on a pedestal stood a stuffed peacock, a reminder of the days when they strutted freely around the grounds. We used to try to pull out a tail feather but being hustled along by Miss Cowherd, we never had time to get one, and in time all the tail feathers of this beautiful bird hung like broken reeds. In the room was quite a large hand-blown pedal organ and sometimes we could persuade Miss Cowherd to play for us, one of us blowing for her. She would squeeze out a few renderings of Gospel songs she could remember, even sing in her very quaky voice, a few wrong pedal notes from her elastic-sided shod feet didn't seem to matter to her or us. We had achieved something getting her to play.

There was also a very small piano, not more than four octaves. It folded up and was then easily carried around to her various meetings. As I could play I was often the pianist at these gatherings. Miss Cowherd also had a Sunday School at High Newton, quite apart from the one at Field Broughton. I know very little about the one at High Newton. We never went, it was too far to walk to school everyday and again on Sunday. When Miss Cowherd eventually gave up the Field Broughton class, Mrs. Ransome started one at St Peter's church, so we went there.

I can well remember the old surgery at Stonydale, although Dr. Cowherd had been long dead, Miss Cowherd kept it exactly as he had left it, even his gaiters were hanging on the wall and rows of various bottles on shelves. These were very gradually knocked off and disposed of by her maids and the room was handed over to a family of bantam hens. "Such sweet creatures," Miss Cowherd used to say.

As time went on, Miss Cowherd gave way and stopped the two servants waiting on her in the dining room. Instead she partook of her meal with them in the kitchen. I have often partaken in supper there and it was the only place and time I had ever eaten globe artichokes. The large flower head still in bud was boiled until tender, put on a large dish, and covered with a large chrome lid. Besides this dish was a small pot of melted butter. The way to eat this artichoke was to pull off one leaf or petal at a time, dip the end in the melted butter and eat only the very tip that was butter covered. When the leaves were all taken, the choke was left bare like a pin cushion. This was cut into portions and we poured melted butter over them and ate that part with a knife and fork. It had a very peculiar green taste and made one's mouth feel very dry after eating. Asparagus was another vegetable grown at Stonydale, and when this was served finger bowls were used of course. Talking of finger bowls, some rather bigger ones were always used in the bedrooms and had a lovely jug that stood full of rain water. This was for face washing. I still have one of these jugs, it is an elegant shape and pure white china.

In my childhood days there were trees, here, there and everywhere, the house hardly visible. We used to say it rained half an hour after each shower was over, the dripping trees shedding showers and making everything very wet and damp. One great Cedar of Lebanon seemed to take up an enormous amount of garden. A sundial reposed underneath it. Humorous lilac and Syringa and Weiligia bushes were everywhere and laburnum hung over into the field.

Miss Cowherd disapproved of horse racing so every Whit Monday she had a huge marquee erected in the neighbouring field and gave a huge tea party aiming at keeping people away from the races. It was a free tea party and very soon became known to the racegoers who would call on their way home and accept a free tea. It was quite sometime before Miss Cowherd realised what was happening and the event closed. Never again did she put on a free tea party.

The family of Cowherds were all very interested in astronomy and had a huge telescope erected in the garden, between the front gate and the front of the house. From there they could view the stars.

## A TRIP TO HAMPSFELL AND HOSPICE

Hampsfell lay on the east side of Field Broughton, Bigland to the west, and what a vast difference between the two hills. Bigland had bluestone and acid soil, everything seemed to grow up there in profusion. Hampsfell is limestone and scarce in flora. The walk is very pleasant, going along the Stonydale Road, past a field called "Happy Jack", and the Scragg - a small spinney at the top of one field, past the periwinkle bed and the roadsides where the violets and primroses grew, on to the egg pudding stone crossroads, with the great stone still there built into the wall, and either across a field or by road to Hampsfell Hall Farm Lane on the right-hand side. Opposite was another lane called Joggle Belly Lane, this ran through to Head House. We took the right-hand side lane and went almost to the farm, climbed the wall, and made straight up the breast of the fell towards The Heaning Wood. On the edge of this sprawling wood grew wild blue gentian, the only place I ever found it, and in the woods lots of primroses, bluebells, cowslips, and dogs mercury, ramps in great abundance, lily of the valley, though this was very hard to find. A quaint plant called herbparis grew in this wood, it had a long stem with a square formation of green leaves on top and a tuft of green and yellow in the centre forming the flower. It had no scent and was sometimes called true-love knot. Another strange plant grew in this area and came out in early summer, pushing its way through the accumulation of dead leaves, it had a pink fleshy stem with tooth-shaped flowers on one side only - hence its name toothwort. A few specimens of wood sanicle grew nearby. Lots of hazel trees and plenty of nuts to be gathered in the autumn, squirrels - the red variety, lived in this wood quite undisturbed, except for the occasional walker.

At the top of the second field is a gate that leads onto the fell. A winding path takes you past Robin Hood and Little John, these being two huge boulders of limestone, possibly left there by the glacier which ran through the valley in the far-gone days. The path wanders on, almost on the skyline to a stile and then on to the Hospice. This being a large square building used for shelter. Stone steps on the outside take you to the top, surrounded by a railing, and what a glorious view. A perfect panorama north, south, east, west having no trees in the area meant an extra good clear view of everywhere, stretching up to the mountains of Cumbria. Hardly any flowers grew up there, some carline thistles didn't seem to mind the limestone, a few harebells, and a few poor specimens of heath. The limestone paving up there was always a source of great interest, we used to hunt for harts tongue ferns in the crevices. Once or twice we spotted a fox stealing around. The homeward trek was quite easy and we had time to pick wild strawberries to take home, these we threaded onto long grass stems, so they were safely carried. The stately foxgloves grew in almost every hedgerow and the small humble heartsease on top of some walls. Even though this area lacked wildflowers, we could always find something of interest - an odd pheasant or partridge nest tucked beneath wild ferns, and chaffinch nests in the hawthorn and crab apple trees.

Back at Egg Pudding Stone Corner, this area used to be known as St Anthony's Cross, we soon reached home in time for tea. In those days we seemed to get better weather than now, and hardly ever thought of taking a coat or macintosh with us. Sometimes we would find a "robin's pincushion" in a rose bush, they were only to be found in rose bushes, and I will leave it to the reader to find out what it was. Feverfew and wood sorrel both edible plants grew wild in this area, eaten in salads. At the foot of Hampsfell was The Farm, known as Hampsfell Hall Farm, an ancient farmhouse with a huge chimney. A tarn near the farmyard where otters used to live and play about in the water. Lots of tadpoles and later on numerous frogs leaping about all over the place. The tarn is the source of the River Eea which flows down the valley towards Cartmel.

## T.V. RANGASAWMY PILLEY (RANGO)

When my father was quite young, there was an army major, Major Young by name, who lived at Broughton Hall, Wood Broughton. He spent many years in India in the army and of course had his own valet. He grew so fond of him that he persuaded him to come to England and carry on as a valet to him for always. The valet's name was T.V. Rangasawmy Pilley (Rango for short), a very high caste Indian from Bangalore.

My Father, always a great favourite of the Major's soon became acquainted with Rango and he was brought to meet us all at Broughton House. We were very young and I didn't care for him touching my dress with his dirty, black hands. He wasn't terribly black but still had a very dark complexion. He often came for tea on his Sunday off-duty and he spent a lot of time with us. He was a very faithful servant and if and when the Major had malaria would sleep on a mat outside his master's bedroom.

Being a high caste, his parents chose a wife for him and eventually, Rango returned to India to marry the girl of their choice. She was heavily veiled until the end of the very long wedding ceremony, Rango did not know her, never even seen her until the veil was lifted. One look and he left her on the spot, writing to the Major to ask if he could come back?
"Yes," said the Major.
So Rango promptly came back to England, Wood Broughton, and his beloved Major.

At that time Father had a very large dog. He was a cross between a mastiff and a boarhound, jet black, and to us a lovely pet, so gentle and playful. He was called Shep and could play football as well as the rest of us. Rango sometimes joined in and I can remember Shep suddenly taking a dislike to Rango, who had fallen, and set about him. Rango screaming with fright was not much bigger than Shep and he had to be released by my Father. Shep became so masterful and difficult to manage and grew so large my Father decided to get rid of him. Dear old Shep went to be a guard dog in a prison yard somewhere in Scotland. He was almost as big as a donkey, two of us could sit astride him and ride around the grounds.

Rango always wore a turban and very often a red coat and one day we persuaded him to take off the turban and show us how he wound it into such a perfect shape. Yards and yards of material and a special way of winding around the head completed the operation and he would smile broadly showing the most perfect white teeth I've ever seen. He brought us two gifts, one a hubble-bubble pipe in which he had smoked opium and another, the red velvet smoking cap, in perfect condition. My brother has the hubble-bubble pipe. He became a very great friend of the family and when the Major died he went into lodgings at Kents Bank. He died there after some years. I am not sure where he was buried.

Major Young's first wife was a very grand and gracious lady. Layers and layers of skirts and lots of black jet jewellry, here, there, and everywhere. She collected dolls, bought abroad, and dressed in national costume. She used to bring them and show us. They were very beautiful. At that time I was about six, not more. Mrs. Young was very interested in Dr. Barndado's Home and bought a baby doll in London. This was brought to Newton School and three of the girls, Alice Scott from Seattle, Maggie Gravestone from Barber Green, and Norah Frearson (myself) were chosen to dress this lovely doll. We all had to do our very best sewing. Agnes Clark (my aunt) was one of the teachers and when the doll's clothes, baby clothes, were all sewn on, it was taken to London and displayed in a large shop there for sometime. Eventually, it was raffled and we, of course, all bought tickets, and to our great surprise and delight, Maggie Gravestone won it. I saw the doll a few years before Maggie died but it wasn't in very good condition. It had been played with a lot so I brought it home and renovated it. What became of the doll afterwards I do not know.

After Mrs. Young died, the Major stayed on at Broughton Hall, servants looking after him of course. Then later he re-married Miss Edith Newbolt from Broughton Bank. They were married in London, St George's, Hanover Square, and had their honeymoon up there. When they returned to Broughton Hall the Field Broughton church choir had an xmas party in the Parish Room to which the Major and the new Mrs. Young were invited. Mrs. Young came in her wedding dress, pale blue chiffon, layers of pleats formed the skirt and a long scarf of the same material she wore around her neck - a very lovely outfit. She was very tall and a great favourite in the village.

Garden parties were held at Broughton Hall, in fact, all the large houses at Wood Broughton had garden parties. Each taking a turn so that there was one every year. Proceeds were divided between St Peter's and charities.

# THE REVEREND HENRY ALFRED RANSOME, MRS RANSOME, AND FAMILY

The Rev. H.A. Ransome was brought up in the Parish of Lindale, he being the eldest son of Canon Ransome. He was educated at St John's College, Cambridge, and took his degree there. He was ordained in 1883 and took a curacy at St George's in Barrow in Furness. He spent two years there and a year at Langpost in Somersetshire, then came to Field Broughton as Curate in charge. The old chapel being the place of worship then. He assisted the Rev. Henry Hirley and then became vicar. He served in that position for more than thirty years and was the first vicar of the new St Peter's church when it was consecrated in 1894. During his tenure at the Old Chapel, a building opposite the old vicarage was converted into a Parish Room, somewhere between 1883 and 1890. In the year 1892 the foundation stone was laid for the new St Peter's Church and it was completed in the year 1894. The old chapel was demolished along with the Old Dame's School which stood near the roadside. Mrs. Thomas Hibberts was the chief benefactor but she passed away before the building was completed. Mr. Henry Hibbert carrying on the good work.

After the Rev. H.A. Ransome had been vicar for nine years, he came in 1886, he married in 1895. His bride was Miss Hilda Ramsbotham of Ilkley and Sussex. They were married in St Mary's The Virgin Church of Primrose Hill. It was beautifully decorated for the occasion. The bride wore ivory satin trimmed with chiffon and Honiton lace, had a full veil and wreath of orange blossom, carrying a shower bouquet of exotic flowers. Four bridesmaids in pale blue gowns trimmed with white chiffon and Valenciennes lace, large white felt hats with blue ostrich feathers. The Rev. M.J. Ransome, brother of the bridegroom, assisted, the bride was given away by her Grandmother, at the ceremony. At 4 pm the couple left for a honeymoon in Paris.

They came back to live in the old vicarage but it was not long before a new vicarage was built near St Peter's and eventually they moved in.

They had one son called Edmund, he died very young, and two daughters, Miss Emilie and Miss Mary, the latter dying quite young too.

The Reverend Ransome was a very shy, reserved man, but he could preach a good sermon and was a very kindly sort of man, much respected by the whole parish.

There was some friction amongst the parishioners when the parish room was to be used for services until St Peter's was opened. A petition was got up and was signed by some 68 souls against having the cross on the altar, also against flowers and candlesticks and a surpliced choir in the Church. This petition must have been overruled because the cross was made out of the wood from the Old Chapel and used in the parish room; flowers, etc., and a surpliced choir also in St Peter's. The small wooden cross is now on the altar in the side chapel. For years it was in the vestry. The Rev. W. Harden making the move.

Also in St Peter's is a small wooden font. This was used in the Old Chapel along with the small pedestal one which stands in the side chapel. After more than thirty years of service at St Peter's, Rev. H.A. Ransome passed away at the comparatively early age of 57. He suffered an attack of pneumonia and thought he was fully recovered, when one day, July 4th, he was dressing to go out for lunch when he suddenly collapsed and died. Mrs Ransome rang the bell that hung in the outdoor passage at the vicarage and drew attention to farmers working in the fields. This bell came out of the Old Chapel and is now hanging in St Peter's belfry, and is known as the Priests Bell and is now used for some of the services. The funeral of the vicar took place on July 6th he was laid to rest in St Peter's churchyard, his grave being as near as possible to the site of the altar of the Old Chapel.

Mrs. Ransome and her daughter, Miss Emilie, very soon left the vicarage and lived a short time somewhere in Allithwaite, then went to Edinburgh. Mrs. Ransome helped with embroideries for the Royal School of Needlework. She, being an expert, was never short of

employment. Miss Emilie took a course in cookery and held classes for years. They
eventually came to live in Cartmel at the Tower House.

Miss Emilie told how one day she went to High Newton from Field Broughton vicarage, and all seemed well at Broughton House farm as she passed. When she returned the whole of the front of the farmhouse had collapsed into the garden, beds and furniture fully visible from the road. Mr Ernest Wearing was living at the farm at the time.

In the year 1937, Miss Emilie Ransome commenced work on a firescreen. The design was by my brother Arthur and was assembled by Miss Louisa Chart of the Royal School of Needlework in Edinburgh. The design consisted of various items of interest relating to Cartmel Priory, the Gatehouse and Market Cross, The Coat of Arms, The Priory, the book, Faerie Queene 1596, Ceremonial Umbrella, Headless Cross, and an ancient Ash Tree. The whole of the work was embroidered in colour, by hand and then mounted and made into a very fine firescreen. It was completed in 1938.

The Reverend and Mrs. Ransome were great parish visitors and delivered all the magazines themselves. They would set off on foot, no car or even cycles, first thing after breakfast, one going one way, and the other the opposite way. In this way, every single house in the parish was visited once a month. If the farmers were busy in the fields, they went there to have a few words with them. Very often the vicar would call at Broughton House and await the arrival of Mrs. Ransome, have a cup of tea and some food, then set off again to do more visiting before evening. They walked miles but were always cheerful and pleasant and welcome wherever they went. Seeing it is such a scattered parish and covers such a wide area, one hardly ever went out without seeing one or the other walking. It was indeed a great achievement.

## VARIOUS ITEMS OF INTEREST

Coal was brought by the truckload from the coal yard at Grange or Cark Station. In our young days, it cost fifteen shillings per truckload, but had to be collected, so a horse and cart was borrowed from the farm - Broughton House Farm, Mr & Mrs. Ernest Wearing living there then - and they would go and bring these huge blocks of coal and tip them outside The Coach House. We all helped shovel it into this place and much hard work was involved, aching arms and backs etc. but it was 'all hands to the plough', and the work was done in time.

However, we all survived and I don't think we are any worse for our strict upbringing. Manners were a great feature in our training, and we were taught how to answer the door properly and to greet people when meeting them. I well remember going to Church one Sunday morning and daring to say "Hello" to a lady, a steely look from my father and after the service I was severely reprimanded, being told it was always
"Good Morning, Good Afternoon and Goodnight." When addressing anyone older than myself, and to remember "Hello" was just not said.
I would be about six years of age. Needless to say I never said it again. As we grew up and the Church Choir was in full swing we each joined after being confirmed, as my brother's voices broke, they took on the laborious task of blowing the organ for morning and evening Services. Concerts were arranged and even a Choral Society. Mr Whinnerah always looked after the stage making, he was a joiner and lived at The Old Vicarage. Later, he and Mrs. Whinnerah and family moved to Well Bank Cottage and lived there for a very long time. A very popular family, Mr. Whinnerah being my Godfather, I think only one daughter now survives and their other five children have all passed on.

After Ernest Wearing's day at Broughton House Farm, Mr & Mrs. Wilkin, their two sons, two daughters and Grandma Wilkin came to live and manage the farm - they came from Haverthwaite. I can remember six generations of that family, Grandma Wilkin was a very old lady, then Mr Wilkin, then his son William (still alive) the other son Frank was killed during the first world war, then William's son Frank, his son John and now his son Matthew. Quite a record I think.

I well remember Great Grandfather Wilkin using flint touch paper and the back of his knife to light his pipe. They were kept in his waistcoat pocket. This is the only time I ever saw anyone use flints for that purpose.

Whitsuntide and Martinmass held Hiring fairs at Ulverston and Kendal and it was the time the farmhands either 'stopped on' or left the farms. They went to the towns to meet the farmers who would then ask them if they were for hire. If they were, an agreed fee would be settled upon for the next six months, usually about £12 per half year, plus their food and lodgings, a shilling would be given to the worker to clinch the deal. It was a hard job in those days, up at 5am to do the milking by hand, no machines then, ploughing by a horse-drawn plough, no tractors, they walked miles a day and during hay time would often work until midnight. It was seven days a week of real hard slogging for six months, then payday and a week's holiday before going back to the original place or going on to fresh pastures.

Another interesting place was Humphrey Head. This is a promontory on the Estuary coastline about a mile from Allithwaite. There used to be a cottage near a natural spring, very near the shore. I can remember the cottage as a very tumbledown derelict building, but there are people still living near who can remember it being inhabited. A man lived there and collected empty tin cans, took off the bits of solder, and melted them down to make safety pins and small articles. He had a wheelbarrow and used to put his wares in it and walk to Sheffield, sell what he had made, and then walked back. In those days the spring was walled and you gained access through an iron gate. People still drink this water as a cure for rheumatism, I have tasted it, but I did not find it at all pleasing. There is no sign of the cottage now and the wall around the spring outlet has also disappeared, but the water still runs. At one time, some years ago, this water was collected in kits or churns and taken to Morecambe and sold there as a health drink.

Nearly all the farmhouses had a "back stove" and baked Haver bread. This was made from fine oatmeal, rolled out very thinly, and baked until crisp.  Very good with fresh farm butter.

Messrs Ellwood and the family of Aysi de ran a Carriers Business. They had two or three very large covered horse-drawn waggons, and operated their business over a very wide area, carrying various loads of goods to and from the stations, from farms or households anything that needed moving was carried out by them.

## GANNY ATKINSON - DOG KENNELS

Ganny Atkinson was an old lady who lived next door to Grandma Frearson at the Dog Kennels. She was the caretaker of the old chapel and went every Sunday morning and night she was responsible for lighting the oil lamps. One Sunday night during a packed congregation, the first lamp went out, then another spluttered and did likewise until the chapel was almost in darkness.

Old Ganny said, "First one of the congregation looked at me, then another as though I could help it."

It turned out that she was to blame, for she had run out of oil, so had watered it down to make enough! The Vicar noticed later that Ganny was returning home after doing the duties needed and not staying for the Service, and asked her why she had done so?

"Well" said Ganny "I haven't got a bonnet fit to come in."
"Oh dear" said the Vicar, "God doesn't look at your bonnet."
"No," said Ganny "but folk does."

Her husband worked in the stables at Broughton Lodge and when he died the old lady had a stone erected in his memory. She had her own name inscribed and a space left, saying she always wondered what it would look like to have one's name on a stone. Later someone filled in a date in the open space with black paint. Ganny was not amused. She carried on being the caretaker for the new Church, as she called St Peters.

Ganny kept a pig but did not know how to feed the poor beast well and when it was eventually slaughtered it was said to be so thin they hung it on the sneck of the peat house door.

When the butcher came to cut it up, he said, "He was sure he saw Great Grandfather Robinson wink through one of the flitches," it really must have been thin.

At the time Ganny was caretaker at the chapel, Parson Wilson was in charge. He had a wooden leg, and when the choir boys misbehaved, would unstrap the limb and chastise them with it. One Sunday morning at Matins during the Sermon, his leg broke down and he could not get out of the pulpit - a three-tier effort - until one of the choir boys had run to the old vicarage to fetch a spare leg.

The discarded limb was found to be suffering from a bad attack of woodworm!

After the chapel was demolished Ganny carried on as caretaker for St Peters for a while. Mr. Squires having been the verger at the chapel also took on duties at St Peter's and served for fifty years between the two places of worship.

## INTERESTING CHARACTERS I CAN REMEMBER

Mr. George Cross lived at High Newton and had a fruit and vegetable, nuts, and dried fish business. Every day he went out with his huge flat cart with a pole over the top and a tarpaulin arranged on it tent shaped, to protect the food from the rain. During bad weather, George wore a sou'wester and black oilskins, during fine days he wore a trilby hat with the dent pushed out, making the hat have a round crown. His dog always ran along underneath the cart. He traversed the entire district, going as far as Hawkshead, where he stayed the night, he was a very familiar sight and no matter where we went we nearly always came across George and his cart.

Another character was a real nomad known as "Old John," He used to call at Broughton House twice yearly. In the Spring he would be travelling north, and in the Autumn he travelled south. He carried his worldly possessions in a small sack, and sold wangs, these were leather shoelaces. He always had a pint pot of tea and food given to him and sat outside at the back door to partake of it. He was a huge man and always looked well and very weather-beaten. I remember my friend Alice Fishwick, and I coming across him lying on the grass, his head on his sack, we thought he had died and were just stealing away when he gave a great yawn and sat up. He looked very surprised to see us and said he was only resting. He was a harmless old man and died in a barn not very far away. In his sack was found a considerable amount of money with a note saying how he wished it to be donated.

Another character was the scissors and knife sharpener. He pushed a wheelbarrow with tools in and when he turned it upside down its wheel was a whet-stone. He sharpened lawnmowers and saws. I have no idea where he came from, but he paid us regular visits.

Another character was the hurdy-gurdy man with his barrel organ. He had pushed his instrument from Lindale and would come into the front garden at Broughton House and stand there turning the handle to give us a few renderings of old-world tunes, then come and knock on the door to collect his pay.

Another character was the umbrella man. He repaired umbrellas and would make one good one out of perhaps three old broken ones. He sat on a kitchen chair on the flags at the back door, one year I remember very well. Mother had put out the old umbrellas for his attention. As he pushed one up out fell a ring, it was Mother's engagement ring and had been lost for a considerable time. Somehow it had dropped into the umbrella, so it was a lucky find and a good thing the umbrella man called. We never knew his name or where he came from, but we will remember him and the other characters.

Also the chair mender, he used to come on foot carrying a sack full of dried rushes, and would very soon set to work to re-seat a rush bottomed chair. The only thing he wanted was a bucket full of water in which to soak the rushes. He may have come from Kendal or even Ulverston, I never knew, not even his name.

1902

Broughton East, so-called in contradistinction to Broughton West or Broughton in Furness, is one of the seven townships of the parish of Cartmel and includes the greater part of Grange-over-Sands, the latter being fifty years ago a tiny village without a place of worship. Formally it was a chapelry dependent upon the ancient priory church, but in the year 1875, a distinct parish for all purposes ecclesiastical was assigned by the order in Council to Field Broughton Chapel, the new parish thus constituted comprising portions of three townships - viz Staveley, Upper Allithwaite including High Newton (in the old coaching days more important than now) where there is a present population of one hundred souls, and a Church of England Day School (now closed,) built by subscription in 1874; and a part of Broughton East. The remaining portion of the last-named township is now included in the Ecclesiastical District of Grange. The date of the consecration of the Chapel is June 30th, 1745, three days after the landing of Charles Edward Stewart the young Pretender, on the NW coast of Scotland. Dr Samuel Peploe, Bishop of Chester in whose diocese this part of Lancashire then was, travelled as in those days was the custom for Bishops, in state from Rusland where he had consecrated a new Chapel of Ease at Colton on Saturday, June 29th St Peter's Day, dedicated to St Paul, and on Sunday, June 30th he performed alike ceremony at Field Broughton in the presence of a large congregation - the chapel there being dedicated to St Peter, whose name in the English Church before the Reformation was frequently commemorated with that of St Paul. The two apostles, it is supposed, having suffered martyrdom together on the same day in Rome. Between the consecration of the chapel, and that of the yard surrounding it, fifty-two years had elapsed. The yard was consecrated for the burial of the dead on August 3rd, 1817 by Dr. Law, Bishop of Chester, one of the ecclesiastical sons of the schoolmaster clergyman of Stavely, who was born at Buch Crag near Ellershaw. In the same year - Scholes Birch Esq of Stoneydale gave the silver chalice now in use, and from that time it would seem that the holy communion was celebrated in the chapel with more or less frequency, but it is a curious fact that in the consecration ceed, preserved in the parish chest, permission to administer the sacrament was withheld, possibley because it was customary for all parishioners, especially at Easter to communicate at the Mother Church of Cartmel. Reference has been made to the Old Chapel at Rusland. Only a small portion of the first building there remains, the chapel having been practically rebuilt in 1868 through the exertions of the Rev. L R Ayre, the then incumbent (now Canon Ayre, Vicar of Holy Trinity, Ulverston.)

Of the contemporary building at Field Broughton. Which during its short existence, had received several additions to its size (notable the building of a transept about sixty years ago,) not a vestige is now to be seen, the whole having been taken down in the year 1892, and replaced by the present handsome and costly church, which owes its origin to the munificence of the Hibbert family. Inserted in the north wall inside the church opposite the main entrance, there is the following inscription cut on gunmetal having an alabaster mount:

'This Church is dedicated to the Apostle St Peter, it was built adjoining the site of an older one, originally a Chapel of Ease to Cartmel, which was consecrated by Bishop Samuel Peploe, D.D. of Chester on June 30th, 1745, and taken down 1892.'

The entire cost of the present church was borne by the late Harriett Margaret Hibbert and her trustees, and by Henry Hibbert Esq J.P. of Broughton Grove. The former of whom laid the foundation stone on May 10th, 1892, to the Glory of God, and in part as a memorial to the late Thomas Johnson Hibbert J.P of Broughton Grove, her husband, and was herself called to rest during the time the building was in progress. The Church was consecrated by the Right Reverend John Wareing Bardsley D.D. Bishop of Carlisle, during the Incumbency of the Reverend Henry Alfred Ransome M.A. on St Peter's Day 1894. Paley, Austin & Paley of Lancaster being the Architects. At the same time about three-quarters of an acre of land, also the gift of the above named Henry Hibbert, was added to the churchyard.

The east window, the design, and workmanship of Mr. C E Kempe, illustrates scenes in the life of St Peter in connection with our Lord's Passion, and is an exquisite combination of subdued colouring and artistic design. In the central light, there is a representation of the Crucifixion, with the beloved disciple and the Virgin Mary on either side of the Cross. Lower down in the two sidelights are figures of St Peter and St Paul, while in the three smaller lights at the bottom are representations of our Lord's charge to St Peter on the Sea of Galilee, the agony in the garden, and the rebuke to St Peter in Judgement Hall. Another small memorial window, also by Mr. Kempe, is to be seen in the South Transept. The organ a fine instrument was built by Messrs Foster and Andrews of Hull, while a Font of Dent marble, a brass eagle lectern, carved oak pulpit, and seats and richly embroidered frontals etc. to mark the various seasons of the Church's year, add to the completeness and beauty of the building.

Four memorial tablets taken from the old chapel hang upon the walls and thus connect the modern Church with the more ancient chapel, one of these being to the memory of the Rev. Philip Knipe, a former incumbent. It was the original intention of Miles Burns of Field Broughton, who may be called the founder of the chapelry, that the incumbent should keep a school, as well as read the divine offices in the chapel; and in all probability, the school was held in the Chapel before that building was consecrated. The Will of Miles Burns, by which he left £50 towards the building of the Chapel, is dated June 14th, 1731, and from the list of Incumbents appended with their years of appointment, it will be noted that the Rev Robert Field's tenure of office dates from 1736 and 1745, it may reasonably be inferred that the Incumbent schoolmaster taught his scholars in the unconsecrated building, or perhaps in the old cottage schoolroom close by the chapel, which for many years remained a ruin until it was taken down in 1892. The last clergyman to keep a school was the Rev William Wilson who obtained considerable reputation in the surrounding district as a schoolmaster, some of the local gentry and tradespeople owing their early education to his teaching. Both he and Mr. Knipe provided accommodation for boarders in the modest parsonage house, purchased for the Incumbent in the year 1813, the school being held, it would seem, as the number of scholars increased, in the large room opposite the back of the parsonage, now the property of the Hibbert family, which of late years has been renovated and furnished for the purposes of a parish room and Sunday School, and during the building of the new church was licensed for divine services. It has only quite recently come to light how the old parsonage house became the property of the benefice; originally it was called "The Cottage," and belonged to Mr. William Slater who bought it together with the large house down by, now Broughton Grove, but at one time called "The Asps", from the Birch family, the latter at that time being the owners of what are now three distinct properties - viz Broughton Grove (The Asps), Broughton Lodge (formally St Andrews Moor) and Stonydale (possibly St Anthony's Dale), all of which are situated within the present parish of Field Broughton. In the year 1809 the Rev William Jackson, the Incumbent, purchased the thatched cottage from Mr. Slater for £90, and between the years 1809 and 1813 re-roofed it, added new windows and otherwise improved it, and then sold it for £200 to the benefice; and the sub-joined illustration is a photograph of the plan of the premises, which was sent in 1813 to Queen Anne's Bounty, and has been in their hands ever since, but recently was sent down to London for identification, which curious old plan, but for the fact that the premises have been sold within the last twelve months, might never again have seen the light. The position of the private road shown upon the plan was altered; a drawing room or parlour with bedroom above it was added by Mr. Knipe over the site of the pig stye, and additions to the house from time to time were made by the last four Incumbents in their attempts to make the house more habitable and withal watertight, but without any very successful or permanent result.

A new vicarage is now in the course of erection, but before it was wanted, on an admirable site given by Mr H Hibbert, close to the Church, while subscriptions are being raised which with the proceeds of the sale of the old house, and £500 taken from the invested funds of the benefice, it is hoped will be sufficient to cover the total cost, about £1900, of the new house. Formerly the living was in the sole patronage of the Duke of Devonshire as Lord of the Manor. It is now in the hands of five trustees, three of whom however are members of the Cavendish family. The Ecclesiastical parish includes the houses at Field and Wood Broughton; Hampsfield Hall the property of the old family of Rigge; the hamlets of Head House, Barber Green, High Carke and Seatle, with a portion of Ayside and Higher Newton. The total population according to the last census being 367. A list of the Clergy at Field Broughton with their years of appointment, as taken from the records at Cartmel is given below:

| | |
|---|---|
| Robert Field | 1736 |
| Miles Dickenson | 1743 |
| William Jackson | 1804 |
| Philip Knipe | 1813 |
| William Wilson | 1829 |
| (Mackereth Clark's Great Uncle) | |
| Henry William Kirby | 1873 |
| Henry Alfred Ransome | 1887 |

It is interesting to compare the above list with that of the Rusland Clergy; while between the years 1745 and 1902 there have been thirty-six incumbents at Rusland, during the same period seven clergy only appear to have held the benefice of Field Broughton, one of whom, the Rev. Miles Dickenson, remained in office for no less than 61 years.

This information was copied from The North Lonsdale Magazine & Furness Miscellany. Edited by Rev L A Ayre M.A.

## BROUGHTON HOUSE - MEMORIES FROM SAY 1912-1915

Living in the house.

Living Room/Kitchen - open fire with crane iron pans and kettle, side boiler for water-filled from a bucket, and ladled out. he only hot water except out of the kettle. Always smelled of soot and iron and was reddish in colour. Food preparation in the back kitchen or living room. All cooking on the living room open fire and side oven. Bread baked twice weekly. Floor bare stone flags with peg rugs in front of fire made by Mother from cloth patterns out of the workroom. Two rocking chairs, all others straight-backed rush seats. Cupboard for bread. Old oak gate legged table. Horse hair sofa in the corner. Four cupboards.

Back Kitchen - shallow slop stone or sink with one tap. Rainwater from a tank collecting roof water. Drinking water from a pump across the road until mains water was later installed. A large iron washing boiler in corner of back kitchen. Dolly tubs and dolly legs. Large wooden mangle. Form in the window with shoe cleaning tackle. Bin for sacking oatmeal, flour, Indian corn for hens. Uveco for pigs. Pegs for coats. Candle bark on the wall for candles. Can of paraffin for lamps, bare flagged floor.

Front Room 1 or Sitting Room - good carpet, easy chairs, mahogany table, sofa, sideboard and mirror, oil wall lamp.

Front Room 2 Dining Room - mainly used for housing elderly relatives in their last days.

Bedrooms - Bed, wardrobe, chair, carpet. No bathroom until much later. Bath in front of a fire filled from a bucket. No heat in bedrooms unless seriously ill when a fire might be lit.

Food:

Breakfast 8am sharp.
Porridge - oatmeal or quaker oats, or maybe grape nuts
Egg, home-cured bacon, or ham
Homemade bread
Homemade pork meatballs - after killing the pig.

Midday meal 12 noon sharp
Sometimes homemade soup
Sunday - Roast beef/pork/lamb, vegetables in season homegrown in the garden.
Sweet - pudding. Yorkshire pudding and sweet sauce if we had beef, or sago, macaroni, rice, or in Summer various fruit and bread pudding.
Water to drink - hardly ever coffee or tea.

Tea 4pm sharp
Stewed fruit in season.
Homemade bread and homemade jam, currant pasty, cake, gingerbread, apple pasty, or fruit in season, tea, rumbutter - special.

Supper 8pm

Variable snack, maybe kipper or haddock.

Food between meals, none unless stolen.

Outside - hens raised for eggs, set under a broody hen, produced all the eggs needed, and boiling fowls. Sometimes ducks. Pigs - two pigs every year fed from kitchen vegetables, scraps and waste, meal, and uveco.

Hay made in the field to provide pig bedding and hen nest boxes. Dry leaves collected in Autumn, mainly beech to help out hay for pigs.

Garden - Manure from pigs and farmyard. Potatoes, peas, broad beans, runner beans, cabbage, sprouts, broccoli, onions, leeks, shallots, lettuce, marrows, beet, carrots. Almost enough to store and keep the household through winter. Perhaps sometimes potatoes and carrots from the farm are bought growing, dig them up and bring them home yourself. Turnips (swedes) from the farm.

Apples and plums, enough to store. Apples were stored in the cellar, plums and other soft fruits, gooseberries, black currants were bottled or made into jam. French and runner beans were salted in jars. The wine was made from various fruits and wildflowers.

Jobs to do - Always gardening, making hay, digging and storing crops, sorting out bad apples and potatoes all winter, feeding the pigs and mucking them out, collecting leaves in Autumn, chop firewood every day.

Sport - High jumping, training for annual Church sports, poaching.

Entertainment - Whist drives, dances, concerts in the parish room - we all took part, singing, magic lantern, minstrels, pashe egging, carol singing. Hunting rabbits by gun, netting ferrets or finding them in stone walls, and sometimes picking them up in the field from "seats" or "sets". The odd fish, trout tickling. Pheasant and partridge sometimes, woodcock. Even a little venison.

Father - Jonathon Dixon, Tailor. Worked from the house, workshop in one room, bench in front of the window, sat cross-legged on a bench to sew, two sewing machines. Heavy iron heated in front of an open fire for pressing cloth called a "goose". Bare flagged floor. Cobblers last and stock of leather for mending shoes, sole and heel. Jonathon Dixon started work at 6 am before breakfast, at 8 am chop wood, feed pigs, then in the shop until 12 noon for lunch, chop wood, attend to the pigs and hens, back to shop. Tea 4 pm, more wood, pigs etc, then back to the shop until supper at 8 pm, and back to shop if a rush order was on. Sit by the fire and read the paper (never a book!) Daily Mail brought by post daily from Manchester, plus the local paper at the weekend. "Mourning Order" whenever a funeral. Everybody wanted a black suit or costume quickly. The suit could be made in one day. Made suits, riding breeches for the gentry, corduroys for farmers, overcoats, ladies' costumes. People came to be measured and fitted, or Jonathon Dixon would go to them on his bike, and then his motorbike.

Jonathon Dixon was keen on singing "tenor". Grange Operatic Society, Minstrels, Church Choir, Concerts, Field Broughton Choral Society, Cartmel Choral Society, Parish Clerk. Also keen "Mason". Great sense of humour and much use of local dialect.

## VISITING TRADESPEOPLE

Field Broughton being very rural, boasted no shops of any kind, so the tradespeople from Grange and even Ulverston used to call on us. There was Mossop the grocer, he came on a bicycle from Grange, called for the order one day, and delivered by horse and cart the next day. Later they gave up the country round and Ashleys from Grange carried on in the same way. Great bags of sugar weighing 1 cwt, would come regularly with the order. Dickinson's owned the Cark Mills and supplied us with flour, oatmeal, pig, and poultry produce, they came once a fortnight.

Langhorne came from Kendal once a month and brought samples of shoes, one of a pair. In this way, he could carry quite a large selection. He came by motorcycle and sometimes had a sidecar. We chose our shoes and Langhorne took the order and they were delivered by carrier later.

Postlethwaite (Billy) was a draper from Ulverston. He came by train to Cark Station, then walked as far as Field Broughton, carrying two great cases of samples of materials and underwear.

Monalee was another draper also from Ulverston, and he operated his business in a like fashion. Taylor, another draper, also from Ulverston.

Then there were the travellers to my Father's Tailors Workshop. These people came from London and stayed in Grange. Rushbrookes and Wheelers both called on us.

We never went shopping. Fresh fish was brought from Flookburgh once a week - the fish had been caught in Morecambe Bay that morning. Meat was also delivered once a week, so we were very well catered for in those days.

Having no post office created no difficulty. A postman's hut was erected in a corner of a field in the middle of the village. The postman, Postie Bill, would come early in the morning to deliver the mail, he always called on us, because we had the Daily Mail sent by post, had cups of tea here and there, and then stayed for the rest of the day in the hut. He had stamps and weighing scales and we were well looked after – a morning collection and delivery, as well as pm collection and delivery. He travelled by bicycle and in the worst winter weather on foot. He would cover a number of miles every day, the farms being very scattered, very different from now where they use their small red vans. In Postie Bill's early days he travelled by horse and trap.

## JUNE 29TH ST PETER'S DAY

## PATRONAL FESTIVAL OF THE CHURCH

This particular day was very important to Field Broughton and was quite a major event. School in the morning, home at dinner time, then get changed and ready for the service in St Peter's at 2.30 pm. The whole parish joined in and the church was full, a special preacher always engaged for the special service. After the service we all trudged off to the parish room to enjoy a super tea - the catering being done by Mrs. Ridding of High Newton - the adults followed for tea, and paid one shilling and threepence per head.

When all was finished at the parish room we all went along to the lime kiln field for the sports. Children up to school leaving age were first to partake. There had been a huge programme of events made up beforehand, tug-of-war, obstacle race, one hundred yards, two hundred yards, pillow fighting, thread the needle race, high jumps. The contestants competed for 1st, 2nd, and 3rd prizes, these were all arranged on a huge trestle table on the field, and the first three in each event were allowed to choose their own prize. These had been bought by Mrs. Major Young and Mrs. Grayrigge sometime beforehand, as they had been on a shopping spree. When all the events had taken place and all prizes claimed, the rest of the gifts were given out, one to every single child in the parish. This being done, the adult sports followed, it was great fun, as there seemed to be plenty of young folk, especially men, in the parish, and they all joined in with great gusto! A collection was made on the field to provide prize money for this part of the programme.

After an excellent display of sports we all went home for a breather, and to change for the dance in the parish room. This was a very crowded affair, the whole parish attended. Supper was served and everyone thoroughly enjoyed themselves. The dance went on until 3 am, so by then we were all tired and ready for home. When we were children it always seemed to be fine and warm on that day, but as we grew older it became variable, and sometimes the sports had to be postponed. One year the celebrations were held in the front field at Field Broughton House, and another year at Barber Green. At the latter meeting, they had a fell race.

## MOTHER'S HOBBIES

Mother used to make pegged rugs to put in front of the kitchen fireplace. These were made from patterns out of the workroom, the ones that were out of stock, and we all helped tear the books apart ready for Mother to cut into strips about 6 inches long and 1 ½ inches wide. These were folded in half and inserted into a hessian square, very stout and strong was this material, and if the pieces were put in correctly, they never came out. A tool was used to push them into the hessian.

She also made lots of wool rugs on canvas and worked different shades of wool into her own designs. These were quite heavy when finished, but Broughton House being large, small ones were no good.

She also knitted socks for my Father and the three boys, also for her brother. Whilst knitting socks she would read a book, something I could never do, but she did with the greatest of ease. She also made all kinds of clothing and helped Father in the workroom, making up waistcoats and finishing off sleeve hands. How she ever had time to cook I will never know, but time did not fly like it does these days, there was always time to do everything. During the summer holidays, the four of us and whoever was staying at Broughton House, would be bundled off to walk to Grange. We had to go to the station end of the promenade and play around there until about 4.00 clock when Mother would arrive complete with a huge basket of food, bottles of lemonade, and fruit. She had walked from Field Broughton of course. We would sit on the rocks and have a lovely picnic tea. I remember one experience we had there. Our uncle, aunt, and cousin were with us and we made off on the tide in a rowing boat, leaving Mother to clear up after tea. Well, we somehow got into the current and had to go right down towards the end of the promenade before we could get anywhere near the beach. We made it, but we had to walk the full length of the promenade, bare foot. Our shoes and stockings were with Mother, so we all had very sore feet by the time we got back. I'll never forget the walk home, our poor feet, it took days to get back to normal.

## GREAT UNCLE ROBERT (BOB) ROBINSON AND AUNT SALLY'S YEARLY VISIT TO FIELD BROUGHTON HOUSE

Robert Robinson, brother of Mary Ann Robinson (our Grandmother).

When we were quite young Great Uncle Bob and Aunt Sally used to come in June for a whole fortnight's holiday. For about a month before their arrival, we all worked like slaves to get the gardens in perfect order, not a weed to be seen anywhere when we had finished. The great drive and circular sweep at the front of the house being a big and tedious job. The day for the arrival, at last, they came by car from Baguley in Cheshire, quite a journey in those days. I remember well the unloading of the vehicle, bass bags, portmanteaus, holdalls, rugs, and shawls. One wondered if they had left anything at home. All the luggage was piled up in the front hall and Uncle and Aunt and whoever had brought them, eventually got into the house, where lunch was awaiting them. A full detailed account of the journey was given to Grandma and the rest of the family over this meal. Then they rested for a while, and very soon it was time for the two who had brought them to return. We were all given two shillings and thought it was wonderful.

I think a description of Aunt Sally and Uncle Robert would not come amiss at this point.

Uncle was a very tall, well-built man, with pure white hair, white moustache, and a pointed well trimmed beard.
He said "no razor had ever been near his face." He was handsome, rather lame owing to a club foot. This foot had been bathed in seawater all his young life, then the best comfrey was used for as long as I knew him.

Aunt Sally really was something to look at. A very flat hat with a large brim turned well up at the back, a feather, and a bow. This was secured to her head by two of the largest hat pins I've ever seen. Very ornate with coloured stones at one end, and a very sharp point at the other. These were pushed through the hat and I always thought, through the very scalp itself. The ornamental end sticking well out at one side, the sharp point at the other side. Grandma used to say "pride was painful," and this, to me, must surely be the painful part. Her dress had a very, very tight fitting bodice, very shaped at the waist and rather long, with lots of small buttons down the front, and of course a very high neckline with collar and white lace edging. The skirt was extremely full and long, hardly showing her feet as she walked along, in fact, she looked as though she travelled on wheels. The hem was lined with horsehair braid. Layers of petticoats and extra large and tight corsets keep her ample figure in shape. She always wore lots of beads, always jet, and even a black satin apron, not like Grandma's white linen one.

She liked a glass of stout with her midday meal. It had to have a red triangle on the bottle,
"Always look for the red triangle Mary Ann (my Grandma), it is the best."
Two glasses were put on a tray and a bottle of stout would be divided equally into each. The poker had already been inserted into the coal fire to get red hot. This ready, the stout was then stirred by Aunt Sally with the red hot poker, to give it 'body!' whatever that was. The old lady was extremely fond of damson pie, and one day ate so much she was really quite ill. Grandma and I took her to bed. Oh dear, what a business getting all her clothes unbuttoned and off, she even wore long black gaiters buttoned from top to bottom of the outside leg. Grandma said it was like undressing a Bishop. After getting her into bed, we left her, and half an hour later I was ordered to go and see how she was. There she lay, her eyes closed, face as white as a sheet, mouth wide open, teeth fallen down. I thought she had died and hurried off to tell Grandma.
"I'll come at once" she said.
First putting on a clean, pure white apron. Then, hurrying up the front staircase, I let Grandma go into the bedroom first. There was

Aunt, she hadn't moved a muscle, she looked as though she had departed.

"Oh Yes," says Grandma, "she looks very peaceful."

We stood there in silence, when all of a sudden the old Aunt let out the loudest 'burp' you have ever heard. I was off like a shot and didn't stop screaming until I reached the front gate. I was absolutely petrified. The old lady had only suffered from a bad bilious attack, and was up for tea. I viewed her from afar for quite a long time.

One of her sayings was "Put your hand into your pocket dad and keep it there."

This being a phrase used if anyone was collecting for any cause whatsoever.

Whilst staying at Field Broughton House, the old couple engaged Beatie Clark and her pony and trap from Barber Green. Everyday sharp at one-o-clock she would arrive to take Uncle, Aunt, and Grandma to visit their many relations. A sister of Uncle and Grandma lived in Ulverston who had a florist and fruit shop there, that was quite a journey by pony and trap, and some of the many rugs and shawls they brought were used to keep them warm. It was indeed like a state occasion, Grandma and Aunt Sally all dressed in their very best, and Uncle with his black suit and pure white hankie sprayed with eau-de-cologne, in his top left-hand coat pocket. Time was a great factor in those days, and they always reached home by 5.30 pm. Every day except Sunday they went somewhere. Sunday, Uncle liked to go to the Brethren Meeting at Backbarrow, but I am not sure how he got there, for Beatie did not operate her business on a Sunday. We, as youngsters liked their Thursday trip to Ulverston best, for a good big bag of lovely fruits would be sent to share with those at home. Aunt Sally's outdoor clothes are worthy of a mention. She wore a trilby shaped hat with feather and hat pins, a very full-skirted coat, very fitting at the waist with a cape attached at the neck and shoulders, a collar also attached, lots of buttons, all this finished off with a feather boa. Very towny really, after Grandma in her neat little bonnet and black cloak. All the garments were black, I never saw them ever wear a colour. Beatie would get them all seated in the trap, then a few sharp cracks from her whip and they were off each day. I can remember well Beatie's high pitched laugh.

  During the fortnight's stay all the best china and cutlery were out for use, a special cheese dish, it was almost as big as a coal-scuttle, which took up enormous space on the very large oval oak table. The cruet also, for these occasions, was a very large chrome container with salt and pepper, oil and vinegar stoppered bottles. All the best articles were out, and what a clear up after the holiday. They usually made their return home on a Saturday, leaving amid tears and much handshaking and many thanks amongst the older members of the family. To us, four rollicking youngsters, it was a day for rejoicing and we almost put the flag out, for Broughton House was going to be back to normal once more.

## GRANDFATHER FREARSON

Grandfather Frearson, William, was born in 1852 at Cartmel. I know very little, if anything, about his childhood, but he became a master tailor and had his workroom in Cartmel at Devonshire House, opposite Ye Olde Priory Shoppe. By this time he was married to Mary Ann Robinson of Field Broughton, and was living at the Lower Dog Kennels, Field Broughton with Great Grandfather Robinson. He walked to and from Cartmel each morning and night after business hours. He had six unmarried sisters, all except one, Sarah, living away, mostly in Manchester. Sarah was living in Broughton House, working as a maid to Doctor Atkinson there at that time. The kitchen at Broughton House was the surgery. The Doctor rode horseback to and from his patients, he possessed a grand carriage, which only the lady of the house ever used. He became very fond of drink and would sometimes ride back to front on his horse, but the horse knew its way around so well, he usually got to his patients. My Grandmother could remember the Doctor very well, and even my Father as a very small boy could remember being lifted to see the tame fox kept in a cage on the left-hand side of the front gate at Broughton House. It eventually died, and one of its feet was nailed onto the Coach House door, even I can remember it being there, it had been painted over many times, thus preserving it. The Coach House was the building now called Broughton House Cottage on the north end of the farmhouse. The whole estate comprised of Broughton House, farm and land in his day. Later when the Doctor died, the farm was sold, but the Coach House still belonged to Broughton House. For years it was used as a store place. Then after 1942 we, my Mother and I, had it converted into a cottage and even lived in it for 1 ½ years. Broughton House was empty and my mother was not happy, so we went back 'home'.

The six sisters mentioned earlier, were called Hannah, Elizabeth, Martha, Sarah, Mary, and Jane. I did meet Hannah and Elizabeth once, they were staying in Cartmel at The Flags. Some of the Frearsons lived there. These two, very severe, and stately ladies came to Broughton

House, they walked from Cartmel of course. They really were a picture, very old world dress with very long full skirts, complete with bustles. The bustle was a very large pad enclosed in a cage-like device, rather like half a birdcage, and worn behind underneath the dress. The bodies were decorated with tassels hanging here and there.

Sarah and Martha we all knew very well. The former living at The Flags, then moving to a small cottage in Priest Lane. She stayed there until she became too old to look after herself, and was moved bag and baggage to Broughton House to end her days. Martha went to London as soon as she left school, learning to be a Missionary. She became one later and went out to Syria, working among the Armenian refugees. She came home occasionally for a month's holiday but really gave her life to the needs of the Armenians.

On one of her visits, she told the story of how a Turk of very high rank had been taken ill, and she had been sent for to cure him. The Turks treated the Armenians badly indeed and were their enemies, but Aunt went to see this man not knowing what state he was in, She took plenty of bandages, vaseline, carbolic ointment, and epsom salts. On reaching his room, she found him writhing in pain and very much overweight. If she failed to cure him she was told she would be shot, if she succeeded she would be handsomely rewarded. After giving him a good look over, she decided to administer the epsom salts. At first this made him have more pain than ever, later, he improved and fully recovered.

Aunt was a very good horsewoman and had her own horse, but the patient had sent a fully dressed and decorated horse to convey her to and back again to her orphanage. The Turk kept his promise, and the orphanage was handsomely rewarded. The orphanage consisted of a lot of small buildings. I have a photograph of them, rather like small bungalows on a hillside, very like Hampsfell. She had lots of orphans and a personal maid. She taught them English, French and other languages. One little orphan I met and knew very well, called Monica Najarian could speak seven languages fluently. Aunt could speak and read Arabic and Jewish with the greatest ease. Monica and I became great friends, she being a fully trained governess and nanny, and working for her living. She spent years with military families and travelled all over the world. Her parents had been massacred by the Turks when she was a baby, she had no idea how old she was, or even when her birthday was. She had great difficulty in getting her pension, and it was only because of her wonderful memory for dates, that they calculated her age and then granted her the pension. By this time she was living in England and had the great pleasure of living in a bungalow provided by the council. But, it was a very short time before Monica contracted an incurable disease and passed away. Aunt Martha had died some years before Monica, in her late nineties, and was laid to rest in Lebanon.

Aunt Sarah was living in Priest Lane, we as children often went to visit her. A very prim, thin, and severe old dear, another old-world figure, we were always given orders to be on our best behaviour when visiting her. Whit Monday was a day we had to avoid, that being Cartmel Race day. My Father and his Brother George always went and then stayed for tea with Aunt Sarah. She prepared a special tea, of course, the best-potted beef and Cartmel fair cakes and hunting nuts. They always thanked her with paper money, and never failed to congratulate her on the potted beef,
"Very good Aunt Sarah,"
"Yes" she said "You see I know how to make it". Not one of the six sisters ever married. Sarah died at Broughton House and was laid to rest at St Peter's.

## MR E SWAINSON

Mr. Edward (Ted) Swainson was the village blacksmith. Always extremely busy, all the horses from the district being taken there to be shod. Unfortunately, he had a very loud voice and used to swear at the horses. He could be heard inside the Church during Service. One day the Vicar went to see him and asked if he could please be quieter on a Sunday,

"Oh no" he said "Thou only works on one b----y day a week."
The Vicar soon left.

One day my Brother Arthur had reason to call on Ted. Arthur was wearing plus fours and the old chap looked him up and down and said
"Does thou go to work like that?" "Yes Mr Swainson I do" said Arthur,
"Then thou's a b----y disgrace and look like a b----y bishop."
He was known far and wide, an excellent blacksmith, his bark was worse than his bite. His wife kept a small sweet shop and we went there to spend our pocket money.

THE END

Printed in Great Britain
by Amazon